COLLECTING
for BEGINNERS

HANK AARON

outfield MILWAUKEE BRAVES

JEFF FIGLER

ISBN: 1470136473
ISBN-13: 9781470136475

TABLE OF CONTENTS

Introduction

King Tut was quite a collector, and I'm not talking about the millions of fans that he's gathered in the three thousand years since he died, including that *crazy* guy, Steve Martin, who came up with a huge hit in 1972 that managed to rhyme "donkey" and "honky."

No, the Boy King himself was found in his fully intact tomb in 1922 with one-hundred thirty-two walking sticks. Okay, granted, he may have had scoliosis of the spine – there are contemporary depictions showing him bent over – but you need only one stick to get around. If you're royally entombed with *one-hundred thirty-two* of them, you're a collector. You know the old expression, "If you walk like a duck and you quack like a duck, you're a duck." Tut was a duck...ah, a collector. And as you might imagine, those sticks of his were beautifully decorated. Egyptian artisans used ivory, ebony, silver, and gold to make them, well... *collectible.*

Egyptologists also found boomerangs in Tut's tomb, so it's quite possible that the young man had a fancy for them, too. I was glad to hear about his boomerangs because what goes around comes around, and that's never been truer with any subject than it is in the world of collectibles.

Many of those marvelous treasures of your youth are worth some serious money now. I'm deeply grateful to my mother for having saved my extensive collections of baseball cards and comic books. I'm sure that on more than one occasion she was tempted to throw them away, but she never did. Many years later, those carefully stored cards and comics jump-started what became my extensive collections of sports and political memorabilia.

Maybe my mother did that because she's a collector, too – of refrigerator magnets. *Hundreds* of them. (She's going to need another fridge pretty soon just for her magnets.) She received most of them as gifts from friends and relatives; and even though she's in her nineties, she can tell you how every single one of those magnets ended up in her kitchen. Did I tell you that my mother was sharp? As the proverbial tack.

But even Mom couldn't have foreseen just how big the world of collectibles would become. The interest in all things old and rare began in earnest in the 1960's. Nobody has an exact date, of course, but from what I've seen it really came into notice about the same time that the first baby boomers were reaching young adulthood. Why did those boomers kick-start the craze? I've given that a lot of thought, and I've come up with four compelling reasons for the surge in collecting.

The Connection to Childhood. Every serious collector I've ever spoken to – and I've talked to thousands of them – agrees that the connection to our earlier years is a powerful factor in the popularity of collectibles. We think of our youth as a simpler time, "the good old days," even if they didn't feel that way back then.

Collectibles are what I call "talismans of time." A talisman is an object with magical powers. What could be more magical than looking at a postage stamp from Madagascar, that you collected forty-five years ago, and suddenly finding yourself sitting at the desk in your childhood bedroom pouring over your collection of stamps, the musty smell of the pages as present now as it was then?

I can still smell the bubble gum – at least in my memory – when I pick up one of my favorite Topps baseball cards, the one with Gene Green's picture on it. The card was green – naturally – and it was one of the coolest cards I'd ever seen. When it came up for auction a few years ago, did I feel a powerful stir of nostalgia? You bet. Did I buy it? You bet.

Nostalgia, you see, is a direct relation – a first cousin, let's say – to the boom in collecting. The longing for the past is pervasive. We see it everywhere. Click your TV remote to *Jeopardy* or *Who Wants to Be a Millionaire*, and it's staring right back at you.

Admiration for Products of the Past. Sure, people say that telephones and cars and tires – to name just a few products – are far superior to the ones manufactured half a century ago. And that's probably true, but what stirs the hearts of collectors are the items that were clearly more beautiful and more carefully crafted in the not-too-distant past.

What am I talking about? How about those linen post-cards? Do you remember what they felt like? They had a uniquely textured surface, and they looked beautiful, like little works of art. I can still remember seeing one that showed a finely built wooden speedboat shooting across the sea with Miami Beach in the background. It's enough to make me feel like I've got the sun on my face and sand between my toes.

Or how about the old pocket watches? I have an Elgin pocket watch on a gold chain. What made them so special were the filigreed covers. Each one looked like it had been done by hand, and a lot of them were! I've never seen a contemporary pocket watch that came even close to the marvels of yesteryear.

Money clips still stir my soul, too. Ever use one? I know some serious collectors who would never part with their favorites. Do I have a favorite? You bet. It has a blue sapphire set in gold. If anybody ever holds me up, I'll slip the greenbacks out and leave that clip in my pocket. It's not replaceable.

Even pro baseball uniforms aren't what they used to be. In the old days, clubs had travel uniforms made from the finest gray flannel, so fine it almost felt like cashmere. Not anymore. The new ones are nice, don't get me wrong, but they're not exquisite.

And speaking of pro ball, the baseball cards were definitely better back in the day. They were gorgeously printed, so much so that in 2008, Topps, which has been making baseball cards forever, reverted to the style of cards they manufactured in 1952, and in 1955 and 1956. Those were the years when Topps put out its best product. The result of their recent, renewed efforts? Fine artwork, fine photography, and fine color.

And when you're at the ball park eating your Cracker Jacks, do you really think the "prize" is still a prize? Those little pieces of junky plastic? Nothing like the metal gems of forty or fifty years ago. Nobody's ever likely to collect the plastic gewgaws, but the metal ones have their true believers.

I'm sure you have your own favorites. My point is that the high quality of a lot of products in the old days is a big factor in attracting collectors.

C-o-l-l-e-c-t-l-b-l-e-s Spell M-o-n-e-y. The right collectible can make you a fortune. Is that *likely* to happen? Noooooo. But collecting can offer smart returns. On the high end, it's tough to beat the Honus Wagner T206 series card from about a hundred years ago (called the "T206" by the American Tobacco company, which issued baseball cards from 1909 to 1911).

Wagner played shortstop for the Pittsburgh Pirates in the earliest days of professional baseball. To say he was one of the greats is to vastly understate his record. Suffice it to say that when the Baseball Hall of Fame was created, he was one of the first five players inducted, tying with Babe Ruth for the second highest number of votes; Ty Cobb led everyone in the tally.

But good old Honus, the *Flying Dutchman* of baseball, leads all comers in the value of his card. Recent sales have vaulted any of the approximately thirty extant Wagner cards straight into the stratosphere. Want a hard number? Try $2.8 million dollars. *For a baseball card.* That's for Mr. Honus Wagner's likeness in pristine condition, but even the Honus cards that have a crease in them have leaped upward in value. (A quick caveat: If you think you have a Wagner card, please get it authenticated. Don't be like the fellow who carried it around in his wallet for years – a mistake right there: it should have been stored properly – thinking that it would pay for his son's college education, only to learn too late that the card was a counterfeit. I suspect the story is apocryphal, but real or not, it lends itself to an important lesson: authenticate.)

I've been talking sports with you, but what about pop culture? Let's look at Bob Dylan, one of the most prolific songwriters of the twentieth century. If you're lucky enough to have the cover of his LP, *The Freewheeling Bob Dylan*, and it's in good shape, you have a $15,000 investment that you probably didn't even know about. Bob (aka Robert Zimmerman) Dylan has just done you a major favor. If you don't have that LP cover, keep your eyes open at garage sales because all the covers are far from accounted for.

Or how about one of those old lunch boxes with the little thermos inside? Remember them? Back when supermarkets were giving out stamps to customers – you'd fill up books of them and redeem them for prizes – those lunch boxes went for three books of stamps. One of those lunch boxes featured Toppie the elephant. In good shape, with the thermos intact, those three books of stamps that were traded for Toppie are now worth $10,000. And by the way,

S&H green stamps are *still* redeemable. Go to their website (http://www.ehow.com/how_4542416/redeem-sh-green-stamps.html) for the how-to. Or let me put it another way: If you're cleaning up a deceased relative's attic, and you find a dusty old box of those stamp books, don't toss 'em. Redeem 'em.

But what's really important to hear right now is that I never advise someone who's thinking about starting a collection to think strictly in terms of its investment potential. Yes, you can make serious money buying a pricy baseball card, which hockey legend Wayne Gretzky did when he bought – and later sold – the highly treasured Honus Wagner T206 card. But collecting should be about fun. Which brings me to the fourth reason that collecting has gone *BOOM* with the baby boomers.

Collectors (like girls) Just Want to Have Fun. With all due respect to Cindy Lauper, whose funky costumes from her pop tours in the eighties have become highly prized collectibles, people assembling impressive arrays of everything from lollipops to Lamborghinis are having a fabulous time. For a lot of us, collecting is all about the thrill of the hunt. I'll give you a personal example. For decades I really wanted a 1953 St. Louis Browns baseball that was signed by the players on the team. What made that ball really valuable to me was that '53 was the last year the team played in St. Louis, which you won't be surprised to hear also happens to be my hometown. So when it came up for auction, I *really* wanted to buy it. But – and this was one of those huge "buts" in my life – it happened to become available at the same auction where I bought a Honus Wagner card. So you can imagine that my wallet was feeling a tad light as I gazed at that long sought baseball. A decade can go by *slowly* while you wait for a treasure like that to come up on to the auction block. And there it was, *beaming* at me. All those autographs. All those sweetly familiar names. Did I buy it? I went back and forth, back and forth. And then

I passed, an act of self control that's important to any collector.

Thankfully, only three years passed before I finally acquired a signed Browns baseball from that fateful '53 season. Was it worth the wait? You bet. The hunt? You bet.

Almost everyone collects something. I've met people who live in homeless shelters who were collectors. The fellow who comes to mind right away was named Joe, and among his meager belongings was a carefully preserved collection of cards. Those cards were far and away the most valuable things he owned, though I doubt he ever sold them. For someone like Joe, I have to think that the cards formed a really strong link to a happier time, probably when he was a kid.

A lot of us start collecting at a young age. Some collectors don't catch the bug until they retire. But millions of people are collecting coins, stamps, lunch boxes, books, Bibles, postcards, fountain pens, sheet music, playing cards, autographs, dolls, Disney items, cards of all types, records, milk bottles (yes, *milk* bottles), military medals, farm equipment...

You get the picture? Anything and everything is collected by someone somewhere. Look around your home. Even if you don't think you're a collector, you might be surprised to find that you've got a collection going right under your eyes.

I'll help you get started, and I'll give you tips galore on where to "hunt" for just about anything. We'll explore the world of estate sales and online auctions, and the more humble garage sale where you can sometimes find real treasures for a few dimes. We'll talk about great ideas for kids who want to collect, and we'll learn how to display and insure your treasures. We'll even meet the King of the Bobbleheads (yes, you heard me right), and a whole lot of other people too.

Collectors who have been at it for years like to say, "Enjoy the journey." What they mean is that having a collection is great, but acquiring each item is what makes it so much fun. That's what this book is all about, too. So I'm going to say right now, at the very start, "Enjoy the journey."

I sure have.

Chapter 1
Get Ready, Get Set, Go!

So let the journey begin! But where? That is *the* question when you're first stepping into the world of collectibles. I always tell people to collect what interests them. Sure, some people get right in there collecting as an investment, but that can get really boring, though in fairness I should say that even before the housing bubble went bust, collectors were seeing better appreciation on their investments than most homeowners.

What's your passion? Answer that question and you'll have a really good idea about what to collect. Just to help get you started, here's a list of some of the more popular collectibles.

Stamps	Watches & Clocks	Televisions
Coins	Telephones	Furniture
Glass & Crystal	Books	Calculators
Fountain Pens	Bibles	Computers
Radios	Prints	Comic Books
Refrigerator Magnets	Photographs	Magazines
Vending Machines	Art	Maps, Globes

Snow Globes	Figurines	Movie Posters
Match covers	Trading Cards	Board Games
Playing Cards	Lighters	Records, CDs
Newspapers	Military Medals	Music Boxes
Disney Items	Political Buttons	Model Airplanes
Coca-Cola Items	Farm Items	Ships, Trains
Quilts	Action Figures	Butterflies
Thimbles	Dolls	Teapots
Mason Jars	Lunch Boxes	Perfume Bottles
Cookie Jars	Salt & Pepper Shakers	Bottle Caps
Die-Cast Cars	Postcards	Mugs

Quite a lot to choose from, right? And that's just a partial list. Let's say you're drawn to sports memorabilia? Even if you're not, let's pretend for a few moments that you love sports so I can point out a few important issues that come into play when you start to collect. You, our hypothetical sports fan, adore the Green Bay Packers. That sounds like a narrow enough category, especially when you look at the entire spectrum of football. But I've got to tell you right now that you'd go nuts looking at all the possibilities for collecting memorabilia from the Packers' illustrious ninety year – that's right, *ninety* year – history.

The same could be said for the broad subject of golf, which on a time line could make the Packers look like pikers. If you wanted to, you could go all the way back to the Romans to look at duffer antiquity. Heck, you'd need Indiana Jones and a whole archeological team to unearth a lot of golf's oldest collectibles.

Are you thinking, forget it Jeff, I'm not even interested in golf's earliest origins? Well, even if you jumped ahead fifteen hundred years, you'd still only land alongside the Scots, who were playing golf in the mid-fourteen hundreds. Talk about a sport with a venerable past.

So in both cases – football and golf – I'd urge you to think about the era of a sport that excites you most. Maybe for the Packers, it's when the legendary coach Vince Lombardi led them onto the field. With golf, you might decide it was when Tiger Woods first walked – and then ruled – the fairways.

A lot of new collectors have a hard time narrowing their focus. Some of them go crazy acquiring everything they can in a binge of poorly considered buying. Don't *you* go crazy. You want to focus, focus, and focus. Don't take a shotgun approach to collecting, use a rifle. Zero in on a particular target, and then let the hunt begin.

Let me give you some examples from outside the world of sports, and the reasons will become even clearer. Royal Doulton makes marvelous mugs with the likenesses of a wide array of historical figures. They manufacture not only William Shakespeare, but a cast of his most celebrated characters: Hamlet, Henry V, Macbeth, Othello, and Romeo. And, as game show hosts everywhere are so fond of saying, *that's not all.* You like the Wild West? Royal Doulton offers Annie Oakley, Buffalo Bill, Geronimo, Doc Holiday, Wyatt Earp, and others. Or maybe explorers are more your type. How about Lewis and Clark, who come, appropriately enough, as a pair? Great military men? The Duke of Wellington, General Eisenhower, General MacArthur, and General Patton.

I trust that you're starting to see that Royal Doulton makes many, many mugs, and has for many, many years. Plus, they come in four sizes: large, small, miniature, and tiny. Almost all of these exquisite ceramics are highly collectible, so unless you can focus, let's say, just on literary figures in the small size, it can get overwhelming quickly. Moreover, when the company issues a new mug, it's wise to grab it fast because they "retire" them eventually, and then issue new ones with new faces.

So decide on a particular collecting niche, and try to set realistic goals. Perhaps with Royal Doulton it would be to collect only twentieth century literary figures in the tiny size.

It's not just a commercial line like Royal Doulton where collecting can get complicated. Even in what sounds like the plain old Glass and Crystal category there are lots of subcategories, including Depression Glass, Bottles, and Art Glass. Stamps? Tons of them hail from virtually every country on earth and from virtually every period of history.

Speaking of history, there are many collectors who specialize in it. If you think you might be drawn to history as well, listen up. Ask yourself, is it American history? Which category? The Civil War in particular (see how we're narrowing subjects down right away?). American Presidents? (I feel like Alex Trebek on *Jeopardy.*) In terms of cost, we're moving way up the collectibles food chain because American history items can be quite costly. Try a minimum (as in rock bottom minimum) of $200,000 just to build a complete presidential letter collection. But if you're drawn to history, don't let that intimidating cost get in your way. Think of collecting campaign buttons from every president. They're not necessarily cheap, though, so look at the price tags closely. In fact, interestingly – and ironically enough – the most valuable campaign button by far came from a presidential ticket that lost: the 1920 Democratic pairing of James Cox and Franklin Delano Roosevelt, with FDR running as vice-president. Value: more than $100,000. Bumper stickers are consistently less expensive, so you might consider collecting the wildest or wackiest ones you can find.

Another approach would be to zero in on a single president, like Harry Truman. You could include those campaign buttons and bumper stickers, along with Truman's books and possibly even an item that Truman owned, like an umbrella.

Trading cards – to go back to sports for a moment – can be among the most dizzying of all collectibles. First of all, there are baseball, football, hockey, and basketball cards.

For baseball alone, there used to be seven card companies. If you collected them as a kid, some of their names will no doubt be familiar to you: Topps, Upper Deck, and Play Ball to name a just a few. If you try to collect every single card from every company, you'll be setting an impossible goal for yourself – and a very costly one. So instead, pick one of the card companies and establish a goal that's reasonable. Here's what I did. It involved a little more than just cards, but I think it illustrates how to define the boundaries of your collection and still come up with an impressive display (the author says modestly).

As I mentioned, my mother saved my baseball card collection. We're talking shoeboxes full of cards, plus bags of them. About twenty years ago, when she reminded me of them, I thought, Wow, what a bonanza. But even then I didn't think of myself as a collector. That didn't happen until a few months later when my mother and son, Nate (also a collector), and I went to the Hall of Fame in Cooperstown, New York. Afterward, we strolled into a shop that sold collectibles, and I saw a Hartland statue of Mickey Mantle. They're eight inches tall, and they were manufactured by the Hartland Plastics Company of Milwaukee, Wisconsin, which started manufacturing sports statues in 1958. My mother offered to buy me the Mickey Mantle statue, and never one to look a gift horse in the mouth, I readily accepted and thanked her. (Are you starting to get the idea that Mom had a big influence on my collecting habit? You've got that right.)

I already owned four of those Hartland statues that I'd bought as a child – Stan Musial, Hank Aaron, Babe Ruth, and Eddie Mathews – so Mickey had some rarefied company when he settled in my home. I quickly decided that my goal would be to get all twenty of the Hartland statues made in 1960. There were nine National League players, and eight American Leaguers, plus Babe Ruth. Plus a generic minor leaguer and bat boy, each only three inches tall.

It was a *great* feeling when I finally collected all twenty of those statues. I had to spend a few years hunting them down. And let me tell you, those eight-inch statues that I bought as a boy for $1.99 were worth considerably more thirty years later. Mickey Mantle alone cost a hundred dollars. So it took a while; I wasn't going to spend all that money at once.

Then I started thinking about how I wanted to display them, and that meant back to the treasure hunt. I decided that since I already had a baseball card for each of the players depicted on the statues, I'd like to get a baseball signed by each of the stars, too. Just his signature on the ball, no one else's. Talk about the thrill of the hunt. That took a few more years, but when I was done I had set a realistic goal of having each player represented by the statue, card, and ball. Though it took a few years to get all of those items, it was a great beginning to my sports collection.

Now one thing I did right from the start – and I strongly urge you to do this, too – I talked over my plans with my wife. You might not think about doing this, but it's a very good idea to have a good discussion about your plans. That's because you might want to display your treasures. Most of us do, though not all. Some collectors don't have the space to display their extensive holdings, while others have items so valuable that they don't want casual visitors to know what's lying around. Then there are collectors who just don't want to *collect* a lot of weird looks, like the guy I know who collects thimbles. Yup, you read that right: thimbles. He does not display them, even though, let's face it, they wouldn't take up much room. The reason he's so reluctant is that he's found that people think he's a little strange for collecting them. He's seen their reactions; therefore, no one gets to see his thimbles. But I like to think of him pulling out his collection in the middle of the night and gazing wistfully at them, imagining the fingers that they once adorned, and the socks that they once helped darn.

In most cases, though, displaying your collection will take up more household space than thimbles. There's also this thing called m-o-n-e-y that comes up. Collecting should not cost you half your annual salary. But no matter what you collect, even matchbooks, it will cost you something, so talk it over with the people you love. Make sure they're okay with your plans. Compromise, if you have to. If you were planning to collect big teddy bears, and that's a problem because of space or money, think about smaller sizes. Ditto those Royal Doulton mugs. Get everybody on board, and then begin your journey, in many cases by looking just south of your proboscis, which is a fancy way of saying that you might have some great collectibles right under your nose.

Take a stroll around yee old homestead. Interestingly enough, that's basically what Debbie Reynolds did. She's a major collector. Big time! In her case, she looked around the "office" and collected more than 3,000 gowns and – get this – 46,000 square-feet worth of Hollywood props and equipment. A little later, I'll have a whole lot more about Debbie Reynolds and other celebrities who collect. Right now, I really do want you to think about what's right there in your home.

What are you seeing? In the kitchen, check out that ceramic cookie jar that looks like a clump of bananas, the one your grandmother – may she rest in peace – gave you years ago. That's right, it could be a collectible. So might the Wedgwood serving plate that you received as a wedding gift thirty some-odd years ago. What about those Winnie the Pooh salt and pepper shakers? (Winnie is still the most collectible bear in the world.)

Maybe like my mother, you've got refrigerator magnets. A lot of them. Sometimes it's almost as if the collection says to you "Hey, look at us. We've been standing around waiting for you to notice something." I kid you not. I've had people tell me that they'd started collecting stuff before they were aware that they'd even become collectors.

A friend of mine said he wasn't a collector. Guess what? The first time I went to his bathroom I found a signed Bob Dylan album framed just outside the door (*The Times They Are A-changin'*). Value? More than a $1,000. What did he pay for it? Nada. It was a gift, and it just kept on giving by becoming more valuable every year. (But not as valuable as one that he doesn't own: the unsigned cover of *The Freewheelin' Bob Dylan* with the color photograph that shows the youthful Dylan strolling down the street with the beautiful Suze Rotolo on his arm. That, my friends, is worth $15,000. *Three* zeroes, gotta love 'em. Oh, and Suze recently published her memoir of her days with Dylan, *A Freewheelin' Time: A Memoir of Greenwich Village in the Sixties.* First edition, anyone?).

So as you walk from *your* kitchen to your bath, think about what interests you, not just what you might have. I'm starting you off on a tour of your own house because of those budget considerations I mentioned.

Now I have to admit that bathrooms aren't usually gold mines, so if you come up without a prized razor or Barbie Doll soap dispenser, don't feel defeated. Move on and scour the bedrooms for rare books or vintage clothing (or pillows), needlework. Blankets. You could be sitting – or lying beneath – a literal treasure.

Ceramics and porcelain can be hugely valuable. So hustle to your dining room and check out that old tureen. And those glasses with company logos? Could be worth more empty than full.

Need I tell you that the attic can be awesome? All kinds of treasures can be squirreled away up there. You have to pour through it. Think of yourself as one of those old time gold miners swishing river gravel around a pan looking for that one pure nugget.

And don't neglect your garage. Remember, Jessica and Todd Moore found the Washington Redskin Bobble-head in their garage. There can be lots of stuff gathering dust in a garage, including garden tools. Yup, they can be collectibles, too.

Garages can be absolute gold mines for all kinds of reasons. I'll tell you why when our joyful journey continues. But first, let's review what we've learned.

1) The variety of items that can be collected is vast.
2) Go with your passion.
3) Not sure about your passion, look around and see if you've already started collecting without realizing it.
4) Narrow your focus.
5) Set realistic goals.
6) Consider the size of your collectibles and the space that they'll require.

Okay, Tally ho and away we go!

Chapter 2
There's Gold in That Thar Garage

Garage sales are where you, the hunter, can begin to stalk big game outside your own private reserve. If you've ever held a garage sale, you already know why the pickings can be so easy. Remember how you couldn't help but get careless when you were pricing items? That's not unusual. Most of us get overwhelmed by all the belongings that we're putting out for a garage sale. Our biggest urge in holding one is to get rid of all that *stuff*, and that's why garage sales are great places to hunt and haunt. But you've got to get out there early.

They're generally advertised in newspapers, or on community calendars online. Some of them start at the crack of dawn. So where should you be at that hour? (Hint: not in bed.) I know you've heard this before, but I'll say it anyway: The early bird gets the worm.

Is the weather good? Nice and sunny? Competition could be fierce. Is the weather foul? All the more reason to get out quickly. William Bates Harding, who started Bonanzle, one of the most successful online sites for collectibles, had his epiphany about starting his own very profitable websites (say 600,000 unique hits a month...and going up all the time) when he spent days preparing for a garage sale in Seattle, only to awaken on the appointed day to a dark and dreary sky. Bill, who's a charming guy and very likeable, found his mood souring when after working all day he netted about twenty-five dollars. He thought *there has to be a better way.* And he found one by building Bonanzle; but it doesn't replace garage sales, where you can see and feel the treasures you unearth.

So don't let bad weather slow you down, because all that rain might just drive away the competition and pump-prime your collection...or give you the idea for a highly profitable online business.

So what are you looking for? If you've settled on a particular item, such as music memorabilia, medicine bottles, or Disney items, the hunt is on. If not – if you're leaving yourself open to all possibilities – garage sales are great because they'll expose you to hundreds of choices quickly. And let's not forget, they're economical, a key consideration. You can also pick up a lot of pointers by watching garage sale veterans operate. The very best ones are smooth. They might pick up an item, study it, put it down, pretend they're not interested, and then say casually "What are you asking for that?" Not, "How much is it?" "What are you *asking...*" Already signaling that they have no intention of paying full price for that piece of ... Well, you get the picture.

That's when the negotiations begin. And that's half the fun. Don't be shy. At a garage sale that old expression – "Nobody pays retail, so why should you?" – is really true. So get in there and get feisty, and pick up that Bogart movie poster for a fraction of what it was tagged. Make out like a bandit. Why not? You're bagging big game.

Alas, when the weather turns wintry, garage sale season ends, but that doesn't mean that you have to turn away from the less expensive forms of collecting. That's when heading to a Salvation Army, Goodwill store, or any of the many varieties of thrift shops will bestow upon you whole new fiefdoms.

Sure, there's vintage clothing to be found, but what about handbags, purses, costume jewelry, even fine china and paintings? Did you hear what happened at a rural Goodwill store in Maryland in 2008? This is a classic story. Somebody dropped off a painting called *Marche aux fleurs* (*Flower Market* for the less Frenchified among us). It looked destined to become another one of those twenty dollar Goodwill specials, except a sharp-eyed store employee looked a little closer. Turned out it was by impressionist Edouard-Leon Cortes, and might have been painted almost a hundred years ago. Goodwill had it auctioned by Sotheby's for $40,600.

What should that tell you? Don't be shy. Ask if you can take a look in the back of the store, go through stuff that hasn't made it out to the floor. Hey, what's the worst they can say? No. But if they say yes, then you get a preview of coming attractions, which might prove highly profitable. More than once, I've been nosing around the chaos in the back of a thrift shop and found my own little nuggets. Nothing like the mother lode they unearthed at that Goodwill store in Maryland, though.

But think about rummaging around elsewhere. How about on a cruise ship? No, I'm not suggesting you plunder the captain's quarters for naval memorabilia – I don't want you walking the plank – but it can be a great place to learn about collectibles. How do I know? Ask an expert: me! I hold seminars on cruise ships all the time. They're so much fun. I get together with interested passengers for an hour or two every day and we talk collectibles. It's a blast. And I bring photographs of some choice examples from my personal collections. See my website – www.collectingwithJeff.com – for my schedule. Ship ahoy!

Keep your eyes on other websites, too. www.worldcollectorsnet.com is one oldest and most highly regarded.

Click your way on to their sight, register, and you can forget about cruising the ocean. Instead, surf the Net. See where it takes you. And don't forget Bonanzle, www.Bonanzle.com, where they say you'll "find everything but the ordinary." Before you know it, you'll be linking to an almost endless number of articles and photos and people. At Bonanzle you can chat with sellers – or buyers if you're selling – in real time. I'll have more on William Harding's website later in the book. He received one of the most unusual promotional offers that I've ever heard of. I'll tell you about that too. (Trust me, it's worth waiting for.)

Okay, now that we've cleared the salt from our sinuses, let's talk about the rather dry sounding business of lectures. Collectibles are such a hot topic that there are lots of talks given on all aspects of the business. Keep your eye on those local calendars. They're almost always free, and they're usually a lot of fun. It's easy to understand why. People like *you* go to them. Lectures will give you the opportunity to network with other folks as obsessed with collecting as you are. It's a tribe, so why not powwow?

Feel like staying home? Pick up your TV remote and start looking for shows about antiques and collectibles, which brings me to a subject that I've been planning to address: the difference between antiques and collectibles. The United States Customs Department says that an antique must be at least one hundred years old. Think of collectibles as newer antiques. Some older collectibles – but not old enough to achieve antique status – are sometimes called "vintage." Let me complicate this just a wee bit by adding that a "desirable" is a collectible whose value has not yet been determined because it's too new.

Got that? Now, armed with that vital info go ahead and click your remote to that huge PBS hit *Antiques Roadshow* and its companion show *Antiques Roadshow FYI*. The original version of the show appeared in 1979 in England on the BBC (aka "the Beeb," a nickname given to the network by

Peter Sellers when he was doing *The Goon Show*. You end up learning all kinds of stuff when you're a collector). So *Antiques Roadshow* comes with an impressive pedigree, and it offers impressive knowledge. My only reservation in recommending it is that it concerns itself – appropriately enough – with antiques far more than collectibles. Nevertheless, you'll learn a great deal of value by watching these two shows, including information about *our* chosen interest: collectibles. And the shows are fun, which is definitely in the spirit of collecting. So grab your remote and give those two PBS offerings a whirl.

But hold on, don't get totally hypnotized by the tube right now because I want to whisk you off to another location entirely on our joyful journey, one that could net you an entire collection in one fell swoop. That's right, I'm talking about obtaining someone else's collection. No, not through anything illicit. This is not *Burglary 101*; or its upper level course, *Breaking and Entering: A Graduate Seminar for Career Criminals*. Nope, I'm talking about estate sales.

What's an estate sale? I have to pose that question for the folks who aren't familiar with them, or have heard of them but are kind of fuzzy about what they actually are.

An estate sale is when the contents of an entire home are put up for sale. I mean *everything* from the cans of soup in the kitchen cabinet to the grand piano in the living room. And, not insignificant to our interest, entire collections of collectibles.

Estate sales are not auctions. They're generally organized by experienced companies that are paid to run the sale by homeowners. Each item is priced before the public is let in. When the opening bell sounds, so to speak, it's time to go for the gusto.

If the sale begins at 9:00 a.m., and it looks like a good one, get there at least a half hour early. It's line up and get ready time. Do yourself a favor: leave the wee ones at homes, and don't try to drag a stroller through the house.

Kids are always getting stepped on at estate sales, and there's no way to navigate efficiently with a stroller in the crowded confines of a typical estate sale. Besides, do you really want to get stink eye from every other buyer?

But there is some skulking around that you can do *before* an estate sale. You can go to a website called www.estate-sales.net. Across the country, many companies holding estate sales upload photos of the items that will be for sale to that website, and in the comfort of your home you can peruse the pictures for days before the sale takes place. Kind of a preview of coming attractions. That's when you can spot all kinds of stuff, including intact collections.

Estatesales.net is the brainchild of Dan McQuade, who was attending an estate sale in 2001, waiting in a line like everyone else, when he turned to a buddy and said "There's got to be a better way than this." What he meant was that there had to be a way to see what the heck was going to be available before charging through the door with the rest of the unenlightened throng. That's when – *voila!* – just like with Bill Harding at his dismal garage sale, a better idea came to Dan McQuade.

Within months he had his website up and running, and in 2003 he went national with it. Dan's seen it all in the estate sales business, and he has some advice for newcomers to the trade.

First, Dan says you should do your research. Know what you're looking for, and find out if it's available. How? Try his website. The estate sale you're interested in is probably listed.

Second, if you're collecting Depression Glass, for instance, Dan says you should study the online pictures very closely. Zoom in on the dining room table or china cabinet. What you're looking for might be overshadowed by a quick glance. Remember, you're hunting. When you're tracking down the collectibles of your choice, you have to be kind of a Sherlock Holmes. What was his trademark?

A magnifying glass. The twenty-first century version of that is the zoom feature on your computer.

Third, Dan says now that you've located what you want online, on the morning of the sale go directly to the room that has the item. *But,* and this is a big "but," don't get so excited that you start wearing blinders because the Depression Glass vase you saw on a dining room table online two days ago might have been moved by the folks running the estate sale after they photographed it. It happens, so remain eagle-eyed all the way.

Fourth, look over the item carefully. Again, you don't want to be so amped that you grab it, buy it, and then take it outside and find cracks in the base. "This isn't Macy's," Dan says. "You can't take it back."

You might be starting to sense that estate sales can become a bit frantic. That's true, but Dan says the more experienced people tend to be relaxed. He says he can usually pick out the new ones, especially if they've found their prized item, and then in a moment of inattention put it down. Once it's out of your hand, it's literally up for grabs. And people do grab them right out from under you.

Dan has seen that happen plenty, but the one memory that remains strongest after all these years was the time he was looking at furniture in a bedroom, and heard a telltale cracking sound. He looked up and saw a woman's leg hanging down through the ceiling. She'd been combing through the attic, and in her haste she'd stepped off the floorboards and on to sheetrock. She's lucky she didn't fall all the way in.

So expect some crazy but entertaining times at estate sales. Lots of people go just to see how other folks live. The one thing you're not likely to see at the sale is a family member. The companies running estate sales have found that family members depress sales. Far too often a potential buyer will pick up a teapot, and Aunt Lilly, sitting nearby, will say something like "Oh, I just loved that teapot. My sister Sally gave it to me, God rest her soul."

The likely response from the interested buyer, "Ah, here, keep it."

But the way a family lived will be on display, and so might an entire collection of Depression Glass, or stamps, fountain pens, or snow globes. There's nothing that says you have to suffer to be a collector. If you happen upon a significant established collection at an estate sale, go for it. If you don't, someone else will. Besides, you'll have a great story to tell about how you came up with all those lovely items, assuming a foot doesn't come through the ceiling and kick you in the head.

I'm upbeat about the future of estate sales. Why? Because one of the chief reasons they're held is when the homeowner dies. And let's face it, none of us gets out of here alive. But there are other factors driving estate sales that are likely to remain strong.

A lot of people hold them when they're downsizing, and a lot of baby boomers are starting to do just that. Their nests aren't quite as full as they used to be, because the kids have all grown up and moved away.

Divorce also leads to a lot of estate sales, as do moves to retirement communities or assisted living facilities.

I've got another reason that I think estate sales will keep going strong: collecting fever is only growing, and estate sales are great places to land everything from a single, treasured item to an entire collection. So don't be shy. You've got all the tips you need now to head into an estate sale like a seasoned pro.

Let's review.

1) Garage sales are great, economical places to find collectibles.
2) Go to garage sales early.

3) Don't hesitate to negotiate at garage sales.   It's expected.

4) Troll at Salvation Army, Goodwill, and other second-hand stores for collectibles.

5) Consider taking a cruise for collectors (I'll see you there).

6) Lectures about collecting abound.   Go and take notes.

7) TV offers terrific programming about collecting. Check out *Antiques Roadshow* and *Antiques Roadshow FYI*.

8) Estate sales are wonderful opportunities to find everything from a single item to an entire collection.

Let's continue with our enjoyable journey!

Chapter 3
Going Once, Going Twice...

Pure gibberish.

That's what I thought the first time I heard an auctioneer. It was *mumble, mumble, mumble* "One hundred dollars..." Then more *mumble, mumble, mumble* "One hundred twenty..." The dollar amounts were the only words I could understand, but I came to realize that a great auctioneer is a true artist performing under the intense gaze of people who often have a lot of money on the line. So watching a skilled practioner of the auction arts can be a riveting experience.

But the best part of a real live auction is being able to pick up a Dylan album cover and examine it closely. Or one of Patsy Cline's. Or a Beanie Baby. A little later we're going to talk about online auctions, but I'd really like you to attend what we call the "open outcry auction" at least once before you start bidding for collectibles online. Why? I'm glad you asked.

It's my theory that if you attend a real auction you'll be better prepared to bid online. Even if you grew up teething on video games, I still think it's a good idea to go out and mix with real people in real time at a real auction.

For starters, you can visit the auction site before the actual day of the auction. You can talk to people. They'll be lots of folks just like you perusing the aisles. You might want to ignore the bedroom sets, but you're likely to find your tribe of collectors one aisle over by the watches. Or by the buttons, which, by the way, are the most popular items to collect. Yes, *buttons*. Can you believe it? But I think it may be one of those statistical flukes. I mean, a lot of people *save* buttons because they might need them; even in our throwaway culture buttons are not easy to come by. But how many people actually *collect* them? Or better yet, how many people display their button collections? Very few in my experience. And I don't think they're in the closet, so to speak, like the thimble collector I told you about earlier. I think the button "collections" are in drawers waiting, in many cases, for a pair of...drawers.

But whatever you're looking for at an auction, whatever you fancy, you may go up and check it out carefully. Glass? Pick it up and look for cracks, scratches. One of those watches? Listen to the soft sound of the second hand sweeping by. Feel the heft of it. Not like those plastic creations that give you only the moment in time with no sense of the continuum, though as soon as I say that I realize that I'd love to own a few of the earliest Casios. Their faces look so uncluttered compared to many of the new ones.

Even if you're a shy, retiring person like me – that's a joke, folks -- you should take advantage of being around so many other collectors. By visiting the auction site a few days early, you'll probably find yourself getting comfortable in a setting that will become charged with adrenalin once that gavel starts to sound.

But let's not get ahead of ourselves here. On the "viewing" days you can pick up a catalogue and use it to guide you through all the items that will be going up for bid.

Now bidding for the first time can be intimidating. So if you're still not feeling totally at home after walking around the auction site, in many cases you may arrange to have a "commission bid" handled for you by the auctioneer. That's when you tell him what your maximum bid will be for, let's say, a 1960s Zenith transistor radio, the kind you used to listen to with a single earplug as you walked down a board-walk listening to The Four Tops. (Remember *Sugar Pie Honey Bunch?*) Then, as the auctioneer conducts the auction, he'll bid on your behalf. You might even get that transistor radio cheaper than your maximum bid. Of course, if the bidding goes over your maximum, you can't suddenly change your mind and start waving your arms madly, yelling "Go higher, go higher" at the auctioneer. That, my friends, would be tacky-tacky-tacky. But a commission bid is a good way to break your way in slowly to the world of auctions.

And if perchance you cannot attend the auction, you can usually arrange to bid by telephone. A representative of the auctioneer will call before the item you're interested in comes up, and then you'll participate in the bidding through him; he'll actually place the bids you want with the auctioneer.

To be truthful, I'd like you to go and register on the day of the auction, get your paddle, which has a number and is what you'll raise when you want to bid, and then move right in there and mix it up with the best of them. The adrenalin rush is just terrific. But I warn you: know your limits. Can you repeat that after me, with real enthusiasm this time: *Know your limits!*

Why? Because let me tell you that it's easy to get carried away. Very, very easy. And when bidders get carried away, that's when a "sleeper" emerges out of nowhere in the middle of an auction. What's a sleeper you say? It's an item that's expected to go for maybe a hundred or a hundred-forty dollars, and ends up fetching more than two or three thousand dollars. That's a sleeper, and it's wonderful if you're selling. But if you catch auction fever and end up bidding way beyond your limit for a sleeper, it will keep you up at night. And if it doesn't keep you up, your spouse's considerable outrage over finding out that you spent twenty-two hundred dollars on a classic fondue pot will do it for you. So what did I say? *Know your limit.*

Bidding does get exciting, in the same way that betting on the ponies or dogs or three-of-a-kind at the poker table can get your blood pumping. Look around you when you're there. You'll see the same rapt attention on the faces of the bidders. Sometimes between all those *mumble, mumble, mumbles* you really can hear a pin drop.

So let's do our review, shall we?

1) Visit the auction site before the day of the auction.
2) Talk to people about the items that interest you.
3) Carefully examine the items for flaws.
4) Get comfortable in the setting.
5) Pick up a catalogue.
6) Consider having the auctioneer handle a "commission bid" for you.
7) If necessary, arrange to bid by telephone.
8) *Know your limit!* (Have I said that often enough?)

So you've done your homework, starting right here on these pages. Now go grab that paddle and take another step on your journey.

Chapter 4
Rev Up Your Fingertips

"*Get your motor running, get out on the highway...*"
The Internet Highway, that is. With all due respect to that iconic sixties rock band, Steppenwolf, the most popular highway these days is the one you'll find on the Internet – and the "hogs" we ride are a mouse or track pad on our computers. So rev up your fingertips because, without question, Internet auctions have all but taken over the world of collectibles, and are likely to remain the dominant force for the foreseeable future. This doesn't mean that you have to be a computer geek to become a successful collector – or to use the Internet, for that matter – but having a working knowledge of the burgeoning universe of collectibles on the Internet highway could prove helpful. Revved up? Let me give you some *fuel* for thought.

For starters, there is an astonishing array of merchandise available on the Net in every conceivable category of collectibles. The number of auctions alone is mind-boggling. A single sports auction house now holds an auction once a month in which an average of four thousand items goes up on the block. And there are many, many sports auction houses. Just to keep up on them alone, I'd strongly suggest that you subscribe to the *Sports Collectors Digest,* available as a magazine or –appropriately enough – at www.sport-scollectorsdigest.com. You'll find similar magazines and/or websites for almost all collectibles.

A traditional auction house, such as Sotheby's or Christie's, simply doesn't have the physical space to house the tremendous amount of memorabilia commonly found on Internet auctions. But even more to the point, it's possible – and at times highly likely – that you'll find items for less money on the Net. Here's why.

There's such a high volume of items offered – and such a wide variety of them – that potential buyers like you and me aren't limited to bidding on a single collectible. Let's say you've long admired Tony Gwynn, one of baseball's true gentleman (and one of my favorite players of all time). At a standard auction, you might be lucky to see a single Gwynn jersey, but at an Internet auction it wouldn't be unusual to find three of them. The principle of supply and demand would strongly suggest that each of those jerseys will cost less than the single offering at an auction house. Having a number of them also tends to keep bidding wars to a minimum.

I can hear the economists out there already saying, "Right, Jeff, but there are more people bidding on the Internet than you could ever squeeze into a conventional auction."

True, true, true, but my long experience has shown that in general – not always, to be sure – you can pick up collectibles for less money on Internet auctions. In addition, many Internet auctions don't charge a buyer's premium, which immediately reduces the cost of a purchased item by about 15%.

So if at all possible, get online, sign up for Internet access, which invariably includes email, and start racing down the virtual highway to the websites that cater to your interests.

It's easy to find them – that's how Google became a verb, by developing search systems that are easy to use. (Yahoo also has powerful search engines).

To cite only one example, type in "Patriotic memorabilia," and get ready to be shocked by the sheer number of websites, auctions, and collectibles available in that one interest area alone. You'll also find the names of lots of experts, including yours truly. If, however, investing in a computer is not in your plans at the moment, you're not without recourse: most libraries now provide free computer access.

When you find the websites that auction the collectibles that interest you, register with them. This is precisely what you'd do when you register with a traditional auction house. That's when they hand you a paddle. In this case, your mouse or track pad becomes your paddle. You'll want to make sure that the auction house is reputable before you take the next step, which is to place your credit or debit card on file with them. Identity theft is a huge and growing problem in the U.S., but it shouldn't be an issue with a reliable dealer, any more than it would be with a reliable auction house. But how do you determine if the website is reliable?

Research. Commit yourself to due diligence. That may sound daunting. It is not. Google the website, or if it's an individual seller on a site like eBay or Yahoo or Amazon, look at the feedback rating that's available for the dealer; it's provided by users just like you, and it will be right on their page. When researching – Googling – an auction site, add key words to your search, such as "fraud," or "failure to deliver." Look for length of operation. I'd be leery of going near a website that just came on board without disclosing a great deal about itself and the background of its creators, because the Internet still has a bit of the Wild West. There's little formal regulation, but because communication is so quick, bad operators are usually "outed" very fast.

Am I overstating the concerns about the Net? I think the answer to that question lies in taking just a few breaths to look at eBay. (see, I told you it would be only a moment). In 1998, eBay had thirty employees and about $4 million in revenue. It was largely an online swap meet. By 2008, eBay had become a Fortune 500 business with 15,000 employees, and sales in the $8 billion range. Sounds great, right? But eBay has paid bitterly for its longtime reluctance to vet dealers holding auctions on its site: the company's stock has lost two-thirds of its value precisely because many consumers felt that eBay was compromised by for-geries and dishonest sellers. Amazon, for instance, has long vetted its sellers; eBay is also doing so now, however belatedly.

My point is that even a big website can have problems. So spend some time doing research. But don't get para-noid, either. I offer this information in the spirit of "an ounce or prevention is worth a pound of cure" because the vast majority of websites with established auctions are awesome places to find items of interest.

And most of them publish catalogues that can be posi-tively lavish in their depictions of the goods themselves. It's like the online auction houses compete to see who can pro-duce the most extravagant catalogues, and that's good news for you because you get to see terrific photos of the items you might bid on. Most of those catalogues are free, and can be mailed to you once you've registered at the website. But not all of them are gratis. Personally, I won't pay for a catalogue. I figure there are so many free ones that I'm not about to start buying them. And every time I buy an item from an auction house, I'm already helping to pay for those catalogues, which I'll explain shortly. But I also have to admit that in my adamant refusal to pay for a catalogue I may be cutting off my nose to spite my face. So go with your gut on this one. Lots of collectors happily pay for them.

The catalogues are definitely "a preview of coming attractions." It's the equivalent of visiting an auction house in the days before the bidding begins so that you can actually examine the merchandise. The catalogues will generally provide accurate descriptions of the condition of the goods. Again, they stay in business only because of their reputations, which they don't want to sully.

Ninety percent of the bidding at an online auction is done – no surprise here – online. You simply type in your bid and send it along. But most online auctions will also permit you to phone in your bid. I must confess to preferring to place my bids over the phone. Maybe it's because I'm a people person. I like to deal with a real person, and not simply bid by keystroke. I know I'm in a tiny minority in this regard, but I want you to know that the telephone is often an option. (If I could talk to you directly right now, instead of writing these words, I'd prefer that, too.) I also think that sometimes you might pick up a little more information about how the bidding is going by talking to an auction house operator. I hasten to add, though, that there have been times when I've been assured on the phone that I'm the high bidder, only to learn moments after hanging up that I lost the collectible to someone else.

That's how it goes with auctions. You have to be prepared for disappointments. Either way – phone or online bid – there are terms that you're going to want to know for online auctions, so I'll list them here.

1) **Consignment.** When individuals have auction houses sell collectibles for them. Generally, the house takes about 30% of the sale.
2) **Seller's Commission.** A percentage that a seller takes on top of the sales price, often less than ten percent.
3) **Buyer's Commission.** Often ten percent of the winning bid, that is added to the cost of the item. (Similar, though usually lower, than the buyer's premium at a

traditional auction house. And as I mentioned earlier, many auction houses don't charge this fee.).

4) **Ten Minute Rule.** An auction will not end at its designated time if bidders continue to place bids within ten minutes of one another. Sometimes it's a Twenty Minute Rule (different time limit, same concept). I've seen online auctions go six, even seven hours past the designated end time because bidders kept raising the price. I've even seen an auction house end the bidding when its phone operators had to shut down for shut eye.

5) **Thirty Minute Rule.** This requires you to place an initial bid before a specified time, if you want to bid during an extended bidding period, such as the one set into motion by the Ten Minute Rule. (Are you confused because it sounds like the Ten Minute Rule? Think of the Thirty Minute Rule as the one that says you must be willing to *pay* early in the auction if you want to *play* later.)

6) **Callback.** You may request an online auction house to call you if your bid is topped. This is considered a courtesy. Ultimately, you and you alone are responsible for keeping track of your own bidding. If the auction house fails to call you back, and the bidding ends, the auction house is not liable, even if their operators failed to give you the agreed upon callback.

7) **Sniping.** A practice whereby a bidder holds back until the final seconds of an online auction, hoping to make the eleventh hour, fifty-ninth minute bid that gets them the item. Irritating, especially if you thought you had the collectible all but bagged, but perfectly legal. You may do this, too. You can even have www.auctionsniper.com do it for you on any eBay auction, if staying up late to snipe is not your idea of a fun evening.

8) **Bidding war.** I'll bet I don't have to explain this one, but just in case you're wondering, a bidding war happens when two or more bidders will not give up their quest, driving the price into the stratosphere (and producing, in some cases, the "sleeper" described in chapter four).

9) **Reserve.** The minimum price that a seller is willing to sell an item he has consigned to the auction house. The reserve (what we might call "the bottom line" price) is known to the auction house, but not to other buyers.

10) **Ceiling bid.** Your maximum bid, communicated before the auction to the auction house. Again, this is known to the auction house, but not to other buyers. The ceiling bid does not go into effect until the bidding reaches your ceiling, or limit. Example: Your ceiling is $1,000. When the bidding reaches, say, $900, you could have your ceiling bid kick in. If the bidding does not exceed $900, you've won the bidding at less than your ceiling bid. If it goes beyond $1,000, you've lost. It puts the brakes on you with the help of the auction house.

11) **Bid Increments.** Often bids must increase by at least 10%. In short, you may not bid "chump change" on items; however, sometimes it's smart to bid an odd number, such as $101.43. That extra $1.43 could land you the item that you're lusting after.

There are other costs that you should consider when taking part in an Internet auction. You'll always have to pay for **shipping**, no matter the size of the item, because you won't be at the auction to carry it away. Of course, if you're having an item shipped, you'll likely want to **insure** it until the sought after treasure is in your hands. And if the item has to move across a border, you'll want to think about the cost of

customs, too. None of these costs should prove excessive, but you'd be wise to factor them into your bidding.

Online auctions are fun, no doubt about it. They can really get your heart racing, but sometimes they're not for the faint of heart. Here's a quick story, based on my personal experience that illustrates my point.

As I've mentioned, I have a pretty nice collection of sports memorabilia, but I'd yet to acquire a jersey by the incomparable football star Jim Brown. I think he might have been the greatest running back ever, so when I saw that one of his jerseys was going up on an Internet auction block, I was primed to bid.

Wow, that turned into a long night. The bidding went on and on. I was exhausted, so I decided to get some sleep. I wasn't holding the top bid, but I was well within range of it. Even more important, I was sticking to my budget. I awoke a few hours later, rang the auction house again, and found out that the bidding had gone beyond my limit. Every part of me want to keep bidding because Jim Brown's jersey would have been a great complement to the jerseys of other football greats that I owned already, but I forced myself to calculate how many bids had been placed since my nap, and I quickly determined that there must have been a bidding war going on. I wanted no part of that. It's not in my nature to give up easily, but I could see that the price of that jersey would soon be going-going-gone. At least a couple of bidders were slugging it out, and if I'd stayed my bank account would have been severely bruised. (See, I follow my own dictum, even when it hurts: *Know your limit.*) Sure enough, when the bidding finally ended, my regret over not having won Jim Brown's jersey was soothed by the painfully high price for which it finally sold.

But let's say that you succeed with your bid. What do you do next? You pay the bill. (Yes, the painful part, though maybe you've nailed a bargain.) The auction house will bill you by fax, email, or snail mail within days of the auction.

On the theory that it's always better to err on the safe side, especially in regards to money, let me say just once that you should never ever send cash. There, I said it. If you're rolling your eyes at the obviousness of this, forgive me; but if I don'l warn other readers, I'll get emails from them complaining that an auction company claimed that they never received a cash payment.

I recommend paying with a credit card. You have an extra layer of protection because your money will be secure if you don't get your merchandise. But there are some auction houses that won't accept credit card payments. They prefer wire transfers, PayPal, cashier's checks, money orders, or personal checks. A personal check will generally result in a shipping delay of at least fourteen days while your check clears.

What auction houses will not accept is reneging on your bid. Always think of placing a bid as signing a contract. If you fail to pay, you're highly likely to be blacklisted by the auction house, *and* your name may get passed to other auction houses that will also blacklist you. Bidding is not a game. Don't take it lightly. Think of it this way: your bid is your bond.

If, however, someone else reneges and you have the second-highest bid, the auction house may contact you and give you the option of making the purchase for the amount of your last bid. A pleasant surprise, in most cases.

Shall we review? We've traveled a lot of the Internet highway in this chapter, but I think we can summarize the major mileposts as follows:

1) Internet auctions dominate the business of collectibles because they offer an astonishing number of items, far more than traditional auction houses.
2) In a matter of seconds you can find your area of interest on the Net by using Google or Yahoo.

3) After you've done your due diligence, register with reliable websites so that you may receive information about auctions, as well as catalogues.
4) You may bid online or by phone.
5) Remember your Internet auction terms.
6) When bidding, keep in mind the costs of shipping, insurance, and customs.
7) Pay your bill promptly. Do not send cash.
8) Do not renege on your bid. Your bid is your bond.

There's a whole new world out there, and it's right at your fingertips. So let your journey continue...on the Internet highway.

Chapter 5
So What's it Really Worth?

The question of a collectible's real value hovers over just about everything I've said about everywhere you'll hunt for your items of interest – auctions, garage and estate sales, thrifts shops, Auntie Ellen's attic, you name it. At some point, I can promise that you'll find yourself wondering what a movie poster or fountain pen or action figure or some other collectible is really worth. It might strike you when you're staring at a rare Beanie Baby with a price tag of $125, wondering whether the little critter is really worth that much money. I mention Beanie Babies specifically because they're absolutely notorious for their meteoric rise in the world of collectibles...and their precipitous fall. See, if you were collecting Beanie Babies in the 1980s, you would have paid premium prices because the BBs were a bull market then, only to turn bearish after years of (apparently) wildly inflated values.

So if a collectible can skyrocket in value, or drop like a stone, what determines its true value? In answering that question, a number of fascinating factors come into play, and they can turn traditional views on supply and demand upside down and send them spinning right out the door.

Let's start with the question of supply, because it illustrates – in wonderfully perverse ways – just how volatile the values of collectibles can become. Classical economic thinking would suggest that scarcity would drive up the value of a collectible, right? If you possess an uncommon German snow globe, for example, you'd think that its rarity would make it worth a great deal as a collectible. And it might. But-but-but, the world of collectibles isn't that simple because there have been many cases where there were too few items of a particular type for it to ever achieve **collectability**. To put it another way, there might not be enough of those particularly rare German snow globes to produce a collectibles market. If that were the case, the potential value of your snow globe could crack as easily as the fragile glass that encloses it.

On the other hand, there are numerous instances where literally millions of virtually worthless items were given to kids who played with them for a few minutes, and then usually – ah, but not always – threw them away. Figure out what I'm talking about yet? Yup, I'm thinking of those tiny metal toys that came with Cracker Jacks in the fifties. But I could also be talking about the trinkets that McDonald's has given away with its Happy Meals since 1979. In both cases, the tiny toys were viewed as virtually worthless, went uncollected by the vast majority of the millions who received them, and as a result have now become items of serious interest to many collectors.

Think of this price phenomenon as a **Paradox of Plenty**, a term that has been used by economists in other contexts. Here's my definition of the Paradox of Plenty as it applies to collectibles: When items are viewed as essentially worthless, most of them are tossed away, leaving the few that remain to rise considerably in value. The Paradox of Plenty is the flip side of what that German snow globe represents –

items so rare that they lack collectability, and thus never enjoy a proportionately high increase in value.

Companies try to manipulate the Paradox of Plenty all the time, but they rarely succeed. Here's what I'm talking about. Have you noticed how many companies have started to promote their mass produced items, even their giveaways, as "collectibles?" But the more these companies try to stoke the flames of collectability, the less likely they are to succeed in turning their products into actual collectibles. Why? (Thank you for asking because I love to explain this irony.) It's because so many people start saving the toys or games – or whatever's being offered as a "collectible" – that their values will never rise much, if at all, because the items will never acquire any notable rarity.

So in the world of collectibles, there's a line between being too rare and too common. Too much of one or the other can have a huge impact on the value of an item.

Didn't I warn you that values in the world of collectibles could be dizzying? And we're just getting started.

Let's look at how reproductions affect value. You might think that reproductions would drive up the value of an original collectible. They're testament, in a sense, to the cultural or aesthetic value of the original. But too many reproductions can actually drive down the value of originals. Say what? Listen to what Lennon Hall and Antiques (www.lennonhallantiques.com) has to say on this intriguing subject. The venerable dealer has been looking at the values of antiques and collectibles for almost three decades, and they've written about how, for instance, a glut of reproductions has clearly driven down the value of real marcasite jewelry.

In the early 1980s, marcasite jewelry returned to style after forty years. Collectors loved the bright silvery necklaces, bracelets, pins, and rings of the late nineteenth and early twentieth century, and their furious acquisitions drove up prices. But by the late 1980s, the market had become saturated with reproductions of marcasite jewelry that sometimes cost *more* than the genuine antiques. Antique dealers soon found themselves forced to reduce the prices on the real marcasite. Lennon and Hall also report that this has happened to certain kinds of glassware, most notably Depression glass, which has dropped in value in recent years because of the overwhelming number of cheap reproductions on the market. In both cases, and in many others that I don't have room to cite here, it's as if the reproductions sucked all the oxygen out of the air.

Trends and fads drive prices up and down as well. In our celebrity conscious culture a photograph of a starlet wearing a particular type of collectible earring can cause a spike in the value of it as quickly as a cheery pronouncement from the Chairman of the Federal Reserve can pump life into the stock market. Add to that fixation on celebrities the almost instantaneous speed of the Internet – where word of high auction prices for a collectible can go "viral" literally overnight – and you can end up with prices no more stable than nitroglycerin.

With trends and fads in mind, let's look at what happened to Art Deco furniture, which a wide number of collectors first started acquiring in the 1960s. All was well and good with Art Deco for decades. But in just the past few years there's been an upsurge in the buying of Eames Era furniture, which initially came to prominence in the 1950s. It was loved then, as it is by collectors now, for its clean, simple designs, which are in stark contrast to the more elaborate style of Art Deco. The result? The value of Eames Era furniture has rocketed upwards, while Art Deco has, in many cases, taken the plunge.

As Lennon and Hall Antiques notes, Eames Era furniture is also an excellent example of how quality – and the perception of quality – comes into play in determining value. When collectibles are viewed as possessing fine design and workmanship, their worth is often enhanced greatly.

Condition is also a key factor. Does an Eames Era lounge chair look like it was left out in a monsoon? Or does it have the immediate appearance of loving care? Big factors in value.

The quality of the environment in which an item is sold can also add or detract from its value. If it's a garage sale – and you happen across an Eames Era green leather ottoman – then you'll probably "steal" it for a lot less than you'd pay to an upper end dealer in Manhattan. Likewise, the quality of the presentation on the Internet can have a big impact on value. Does the photograph of the ottoman (in this case) make it look appealing? Is the ottoman's provenance, as dealers refer to a collectible's origins, clearly stated? For that matter, is the writing about the ottoman crisp and clean? And don't forget the seller's feedback rating because it can have an impact on price – value, that is – too. Buyers are far less likely to fork over a dime more than necessary to a dealer with negative feedback.

Collectors can also find themselves squeezing pennies because of tough economic times. Let's take a look at the value of the good old greenback and its impact. If the U.S. dollar shrinks in value, it will inflate the costs of collectibles from abroad, but shrinking dollars will also drive up the prices on American collectibles, popular in Europe or Asia. That's great if you're selling, but tough if you're collecting. It's easy to see that globalization applies to the world of collectibles as much as it does to anything.

Then there's the undeniable impact of a recession, but even a battered economy can have a paradoxical impact on the value of collectibles. How's that, you say? Don't collectors – like everyone else – watch their spending in tough economic times? Yes, they do, but what may be even more noteworthy is that collectors generally spend their money differently when the Dow dips. To be sure, spending on luxuries tends to fall in a weak economy, but fewer people move, so that often means that they spend more on their existing homes. This can actually spark the sale of collectibles, a development that many dealers have noted through one economic cycle after another.

But you don't have to be an economist or hold an MBA to be a savvy collector. There are lots of price guides out there that can give you ballpark values for collectibles, but let me quickly caution you not to put too much faith in them. Always remember that they're *guides,* after all. By the time they're published, they can be outdated. Now, having struck this cautionary note let me hasten to add that getting ballpark figures helps many collectors, especially newcomers. With that in mind, by all means look at *Kovels' Antiques and Collectibles Price Guide* for the most recent year available. A typical Kovels' guide will list prices, descriptions, and year of sales for about 600,000 collectibles. *Warman's Antiques and Collectibles* is another guide to the values of collectibles that's definitely worth looking at. As I say, there are many guides available, but I'd be remiss if I didn't mention at least one more excellent source: *Miller's Antiques and Collectibles.* All three of these guides have a strong online presence, with websites dedicated to educating collectors. They offer online video presentations as well, so visit their websites and use their guides. They'll get you into the ballpark, and that's a good place to start.

There are also guides for specific categories. An excellent example is *Price Guide to American Patriotic Memorabilia* by Michael Pollok. Other collectible categories have similar guides. And websites abound. Just Google your collectible of choice and get ready to click.

As we've seen, *lots* of factors affect value. Let's review them to make sure this sometimes complicated realm remains as simple and clear as possible.

1) Items must possess rarity to have value, but if they are too rare they cannot achieve **collectability.**
2) Companies that try to promote the collectability of mass-produced items rarely succeed because too many people are lured into hoarding them.
3) Reproductions can drive down the value of original collectibles.
4) Quality affects value. So does an item's condition.
5) Sales environment also affects value.
6) In a global marketplace, the value of the U.S. dollar can have a big impact on the worth of collectibles.
7) Economic conditions in the U.S. and abroad also affect the value of collectibles.
8) Price guides can give you ballpark values.

To be forewarned is to be forearmed. Never has this expression been truer than in the world of collectibles. Now that we've armed ourselves, let's take our joyful journey to an innovative new website where buyers and sellers of collectibles work out the value of their items directly with one another in real time. It's a step beyond auctions or anything else that we've talked about so far, and it's as intriguing as it is fascinating. Then we'll move into the glitzy realm of collectibles, celebrities, and the bewildering blending of both.

Chapter 6
Garage Sale Meets Gamer

Bonanzle started up online in June of 2008, and quickly became a favorite of collectors everywhere. It's the brainchild of William Bates Harding. You may recall that I introduced Bill to you briefly a few chapters back. He's a lean, fair-haired guy with the warmest smile. .

A few years ago, Bill decided to move from his apartment, and like so many of us he found that he was, once again, about to lug a dozen boxes packed with stuff to his new digs – things that he hadn't even looked at in years. He found himself wondering what was in those old boxes, so he took a gander and decided to hold a garage sale.

Bill's a meticulous guy, which is obvious when you visit www.Bonanzle.com. It was also obvious if you went to his garage sale. He'd spent days carefully pricing and tagging every last item. He lived in Seattle, so he'd planned the event for a Saturday morning. He figured his chance of hitting it just right with the weather was good. Real good. It was August, after all, and even in Seattle, August is usually beautiful and, well, if not sunny, at least not torrential.

The big day dawned...kind of. Actually, the sky was dark. Really dark. "A very bad omen," Bill said.

Then it started to rain. It didn't just rain, it poured. It was like every seam in the sky had exploded. As Bill watched those big fat raindrops smack against his driveway and drain to the street, he saw his best laid plans washing away. Not to mention potential profits.

Oh, he tried to make light of it. He even put on Hawaiian music and a face as bright as the tropics. But at the end of the day, 80% of what had been in those boxes was still unsold, and Bill had all of twenty-five dollars in his pocket to show for his efforts. He reviewed these dismal developments, "And then I decided that there had to be a better way to sell stuff."

No, he wasn't tempted to go to eBay or craigslist or any other site. He wanted something better than anything on the Web; something simpler, faster, more personal. And he thought, not immodestly, that he was just the guy to come up with it. Why? Because Bill had worked as a video game programmer for years. Yup, that's right, if your kid has eyes that are all but crossed from staring at *Pokémon* or *Super Mario Brothers* for hours on end, Bill was one of the guys at Nintendo who was responsible for his condition. He knew a great deal about the value of **interactivity** from his background in video games, the critical importance that "gamers," as they're known, place on the ability to interact with their virtual worlds. Bill had noticed that interactivity was mostly lacking on existing sites catering to collectors. So he set out to change all that. And he has.

When he launched his website he made it possible for a collector visiting Bonanzle to sign up and make a purchase in under a minute. Yes, you read that right: *under a minute*. No long drawn out process that leaves your fingertips numb by the time you've entered all the information demanded by other, well known sites. When you go to Bonanzle, you get photos of collectibles, descriptions, and comparative prices as fast as *click-click-click*. Speed, as every good gamer knows, is critical. We're not playing Atari's *Pong* anymore (unless, of course, we're collecting the vintage models).

But just as important to Bill's success was the ease with which collectors could list their items for sale. As many of you know, the process at eBay or other sites can be dauntingly complex. It's not unusual to have to plow through seven or more screens just to pick out a category for your item. Not at Bonanzle. Try one screen on, and the "advanced" link yields up two more lines. Simple? You bet. But the advantages don't stop with simplicity itself.

When you list your goods, you can also search Amazon and Yahoo for descriptions of your collectibles – right from the listing screen. And the system Bill's devised will also give you the average selling prices for goods that match the ones you want to sell.

It's also super simple to add pictures of your collectibles, and then crop them. Bill's commissions on sold items are in the 3-5% range, roughly a half to a third of eBay. And he came up with a catchy slogan: "Find everything but the ordinary."

So what has Bill found? Fans. Millions of them. Collectors flocked to Bonanzle. They can find a huge array of non-generic collectibles, everything from jewelry, watches, clothing, glassware, pottery, decorative items, holiday and seasonal goods, toys, handbags, cookie jars, boots, shoes, black Americana, rare books and magazines, and a whole lot more. Thousands of items.

Within a year, Bonanzle was up to three quarters of a million unique visitors a month, which has launched him into third place among non-eBay sites. By the time you read this, I strongly suspect that Bill's Bonanzle will have moved much higher. He hasn't done it with any high-priced advertising, either. "Our growth has been ad hoc and grass roots all the way," Bill said during one of the most congenial talks I've had in a long time.

A big reason Bonanzle is so successful is that Bill has made the impersonal world of Internet sales, personal. He's done this by allowing buyers and sellers to "chat" to one another in real time. You can ask about a collectible's history, figure out a pick-up time, or how you want the item shipped. And you can negotiate. In that sense, it's a lot like a garage sale, but without all the driving around. You don't like the price, you counter. The buyer counters. It's like you're haggling right there by the oil stains on a driveway. And there are auctions on Bonanzle as well.

If you're selling, you can also choose to receive instant messages (IM) from Bonanzle. That's a great advantage for buyers as well because it can sweep you right into real time talk with the seller about the item you want to buy. The heck with delays. This is the age of instant messaging!

Why aren't these technological leaps standard-issue everywhere? I'll let the expert answer that.

"If you want to have chat on your website," Bill said, "you have to have to be able to handle ten times the load." By that he means that a computer system for a website with chat has to be prepared to be seriously challenged. During Bonanzle's "beta launch" (think of it as a trial run with public participation), Bonanzle had a few headaches; but Bill and his team found the technological Tylenol, and things have been running smoothly ever since.

As for me, do you think I'm drinking Bonanzle's Kool-Aid because my praise is so high? No way. I'd never claim to be an expert on the Internet, but the folks who run www. ecommerce-guide.com certainly are, and here's what they have to say about Bonanzle:

"An eBay alternative that is quite simply, the best I've seen in my four years of reviewing and writing about start-up marketplaces aimed at taking sellers away from eBay."

Though Bonanzle is still quite young, even by the accelerating age standards of the Internet, Bill's had a few funny encounters along the way. Among his favorites was an email that he received regarding potential advertising for Bonanzle. I'll let Bill pick up the story from here:

"It was from a guy, and he said that he understood that we do word-of-mouth advertising, and that we planned on using more traditional ads as our business grew. All of which was true. Then he offered to have the back of his hands tattooed with 'Bonanzle.' He said the 'dot com' would appear right below the company name. He was quite specific, too. He said that when he made a fist, the dot com would 'bottom out at about a half inch from my knuckles,' and that the letters would be approximately one-inch square blocks in boldface. He said he lived in a 'worldwide tourist community,' and that the price for the ad on one hand would be $2,500. $4,500 for both hands."

Such a deal! And Bill said that the guy had offered to even throw in interviews with the media "at no additional charge."

Bill passed on the offer. I'd have to think that using one of humankind's oldest media – inked skin – to sell one of the most cutting edge websites for collectors wasn't consistent with Bonanzle's overall image.

So let's look at the Bonanzle highlights, shall we?

1) A rainy day led to a new website that may *reign* supreme someday soon.
2) Bill applied **interactivity** from the furiously paced world of video games to a website that quickly became popular with collectors.
3) In addition to speed, Bonanzle made buying and selling for collectors simple.
4) Buyers and sellers can talk to each other in "real time," which produces an experience as close to a garage sale as you can get, short of driving around.

5) Bonanzle went viral by word-of-mouth, but rejected the use of a far less metaphorical reference to human anatomy: skin. (As Bill said, "If that's not a sign of the economic times, I don't know what is!")

One sign of our times is the intense interest in celebrity collectibles, everything from modestly priced items to the baubles that define "the sky's the limit." It's gossipy, gorgeous, and filled with fascinating goods. And it's the next step on our joyful journey.

Chapter 7
Celebrities and Collectibles

Who's a celebrity? Michael Jordan? We don't really have to ask about the man who gave hang time a whole new meaning, do we? But what about famous fictional characters, like Harry Potter, who exist only in our minds? Or Winnie the Pooh, who after more than eighty years, still reigns supreme over bedroom kingdoms the world over?

In the world of collectibles, the answer to who is a celebrity can be answered by looking at what gets collected. With that in mind, let's turn our attention to a pair of slippers. A very special pair of ruby red slippers reputed to have magical powers in one of the most memorable films of all time. Some of you might have guessed already, I'm sure. I'm talking about the marvelous red slippers that Dorothy wore in 1939 in *The Wizard of Oz.*" Talk about a collectible!

MGM, which made the movie, auctioned off a pair of them in 1970 for $15,000. A hefty price for slippers, but not outlandish for *these* slippers. But as the years unfolded, that figure wouldn't even amount to a down payment on the other slippers in Dorothy's closet. Say what? There were eight pairs of the size five slippers made for the movie. That's what film historians believe, though no one's absolutely sure.

Back to that auctioned pair for a moment. It was donated to the Smithsonian Institute in 1979, where they've rested quietly ever since, far from the slipper frenzy that followed. Now, I'd like you to follow the trail of just one other pair. Christie's East auctioned them for $165,000 in 1988. Twelve years later, the guy who bought them from Christie's had them auctioned again, and they went for $666,000 – more than half a million dollars in appreciation. Now that's celebrity star power. Remember, we're talking about a pair of slippers here.

Maybe you're reading this thinking, that's great, Jeff, but I'm not going to pop for a $666,000 pair of slippers. Get real. Okay, I hear you (or as President Clinton used to say, "I feel your pain.") but I bring this up for a few telling reasons. Dorothy's slippers demonstrate the immensely profitable convergence of celebrities and the objects that are associated with them. Some of those items, as with the highly esteemed slippers worn on Judy Garland's tiny feet, have become cultural icons. And while even $15,000 is a lot to spend on slippers, Dorothy's little red numbers have possessed astonishing investment potential. Witness that $666,000 sale. But there's another reason, and it goes straight to the heart of the treasure hunter in all of us, from veteran collectors to anyone reading this book with an eye to getting started on their newest passion: the scampering after Dorothy's slippers *is not over.* That's right. Remember that I said that film historians believe that eight pairs of the ruby red slippers were made for the film? Not all of them have been accounted for, which is why those red slippers have long been known as the "Holy Grail of Hollywood." So keep your eyes open because, as I say, this hunt continues, as it does for long lost items throughout the world of collectibles.

From the same era as *The Wizard of Oz,* let's consider *The Maltese Falcon,* more specifically the statue of the bird itself. It was depicted in the film as a long-lost treasure dating back to 1539, when the Knights Templar of Malta paid tribute to Charles V of Spain. Whatever a real statue of a Maltese falcon might have been worth in the sixteenth century would undoubtedly have paled compared to the value of the one in the film to Gary Milan, a retired Los Angeles dentist. Dr. Milan bought the bird for $400,000 in the mid-1980s, replete with a bent tail feather, reportedly caused when actress Lee Patrick dropped the falcon on Bogart. It also has slash marks, apparently the result of actor Sydney Greenstreet's efforts to scrape the paint off the falcon with a knife in a key scene.

If – more likely *when* – the falcon flies again at an auction or private sale, I'd bet the bank on it going for a whole lot more than Dr. Milan paid for it. Only two of the birds were made for the film (eleven inches tall, but a hefty, leaden fifty pounds – Bogart's lucky he survived the bird's fall), which makes Dorothy's slippers seem almost mass produced by comparison.

Props and costumes have long histories as collectibles. In recent years, a complete Roman officer's costume from *Ben Hur* sold for $5,500. A wool skirt worn by Ingrid Bergman in *Casablanca* fetched $7,500. Or how about $12,000 for an off-white hat with an upturned brim and elastic straps, sported by Vivien Leigh in *Gone With the Wind?*" A black felt English mariner's hat worn by Marlon Brando in *Mutiny on the Bounty* sold for $4,000, and one of the six sets of tablets of the Ten Commandments for the movie of the same name went for $10,000 – or about a grand for each commandment. You could have even furnished your fanny with a first-class dining room chair from *Titanic* for a mere $2,250 (no word on whether Kate or Lenny warmed it up first).

Here's a list of other intriguing Hollywood memorabilia that I've put together.

A Few Good Men. White officer's uniform cap worn by Tom Cruise: $1,600.

Amityville Horror. Realty sign used in the 1979 film: $330.

Armageddon. Space helmet worn by Bruce Willis: $2,500.

Batman Forever. Elbow-length silver gloves worn by Val Kilmer: $1,600.

Birth of a Nation. Metal bayonet with a canvas and leather backpack: $650.

Bonnie and Clyde. Button-front linen dress worn by Faye Dunaway: $6,000.

Bull Durham. Wilson baseball glove worn by Susan Sarandon: $600.

Camelot. Two-piece wool gown worn by Vanessa Redgrave: $2,000.

Cleopatra. Egyptian-style crown worn by Elizabeth Taylor: $9,500.

Cool Hand Luke. Wooden cane carried by Boss Godfrey: $1,600.

Forrest Gump. Box of chocolates and a baseball cap, both signed by Tom Hanks: $3,075.

Gladiator. Arena helmet made of fiberglass: $1,200.

Grease. Black and white saddle shoes and yellow bobby socks worn by Olivia Newton-John: $8,000.

Indiana Jones and the Temple of Doom. Leather wrapped wooden handle: $850.

Jurassic Park. Original folder promoting the park, used as a prop in the film: $360.

Little Woman. Brown silk skirt and a gold blouse, worn by Katherine Hepburn: $10,000.

Mission Impossible. Custom-made "gadget" gun used by Jon Voight: $4,000.

Patton. Green wool military shirt worn by George C. Scott: $3,575.

Romeo and Juliet. Period pants worn by Leslie Howard in the 1936 film: $650.

Spartacus. Flat metal battle sword with metal helmet worn by the Roman
Legionnaires: $2,500.

Star Wars. Storm trooper helmet used in *The Empire Strikes Back* and *Return of*
the Jedi: $45,111.

The Alamo . Full-size Mexican flag: $950.

The Man Who Shot Liberty Valance. Navy blue wool bib-front shirt worn by
John Wayne: $7,000.

The Mask of Zorro. Cape worn by Antonio Banderas: $330.

The Natural. Original Knights jacket worn by Robert Redford: $4,235.

Snippets – and I use that term advisedly – of the films themselves have also sold for hefty sums. Try a single cell (a frame in a cartoon) from the original *Snow White* for $209,000, topped by a cell from Donald Duck's *Orphan's Benefit* for almost $300,000.

With those kinds of numbers flying around, maybe we should look at collecting movie posters, which can be much less costly. You can buy them for ten bucks or less, and take pleasure in the extraordinary design and artistic skills that go into making them. Then you could try to get them signed by the stars, which definitely ups their value. Or...you can buy posters already signed; on the old price ladder you're still going to find yourself considerably south of those props and costumes that I've been talking about.

Posters can be a blast. Did you like Roger Moore as 007? You can pick up a poster of *For Your Eyes Only* for less than $200, and it'll have his signature along with other members of the cast. Most dealers selling signed posters will also provide a **Certificate of Authenticity**, known as a **COA**, along with a detailed description of the poster's condition. There are tons of signed posters available. In the same price range you can pick up *3:10 To Yuma* with the autographs of Russell Crowe, Gretchen Moil, and Christian Baile, or *A Clockwork Orange* with the rarified scratching of Malcolm McDowell, Warren Clarke, John Clive and Miriam Karlin. Signed or unsigned, posters are a great way to own marvelous representations of Hollywood without breaking the bank.

Generally speaking, these are the major criteria for determining the value of posters:

1) **Visual appeal.** The poster should be a piece of art, blending color, light, and shade.

2) **Age.** This can be critical in appraising a poster. The older the poster, the fewer there will be of any particular piece. The history of the era can be a big price factor, too: during World War II, posters often were recycled to make more paper, further forcing down the number of posters available…and of course driving up their prices.

3) **Actors.** The posters featuring Marilyn Monroe, Humphrey Bogart, Lauren Bacall, Sylvester Stallone, Marlin Brando, Clark Cable, Rudy Valentino, and Judy Garland are extremely valuable, even if the movies depicted in the posters weren't chart busters.

4) **The films.** Famous ones, such as *Citizen Kane, Gone with the Wind, King Kong, Titanic, The Ten Commandments, The Wizard of Oz, and Casablanca,* command top prices.

5) **Condition.** Get the COA, and look for creases, tears, holes, stains, markings, tape, and trimming. Also, step

back and see if the poster has faded. You want true color.

Now I don't want you to get the impression that all posters are modeslly priced. An original poster for *Casablanca* or *The Maltese Falcon* could easily cost $50,000. A *King Kong* poster from 1933 sold for $51,200 at a Christie's auction. But the granddaddy of all poster sales goes to the one made for...(open the envelope, please) the *Mummy* in 1932. It sold for $453,500 at Sotheby's.

Relax, Baby Boomers, because a poster for the Beatles *Help* or *Yellow Submarine* will prove far more affordable at prices of a $1,000 to $1,500. Hardly cheap, but at least those prices aren't stratospheric.

A poster's value is helped if the movie was a hit, and even more so if the poster depicts a famous scene from the film. For example, the poster of Gene Kelly, Donald O'Connor and Debbie Reynolds dancing in *Singing in the Rain* sells for about $2,500. Similarly, a poster featuring the mugs of one or more top stars will command big dollars. For instance, the one showing Katherine Hepburn and Cary Grant from their 1938 movie *Bringing up Baby* sells for several thousand dollars. So does the one that shows Marilyn Monroe in her most famous scene in *The Seven Year Itch* (Monroe, in an ecstasy of effort, tries to hold down the whipped up hem of her white dress. *Now* you remember.).

The takeaway message here is that posters have a huge price spectrum, which includes modestly priced, entry level collectibles. Regardless of what you spend, invest wisely. There are great resources for tracking the costs of movie posters. *Big Reel* (Krause Publications) and/or *Movie Collectors World* (Arena Publication Company) are publications well worth a subscription. A couple of books of note are *Movie Poster Prices* by Jon Warren, and *Poster Price Alliance* by John Kisch.

Any discussion of celebrities has to pay attention to Hollywood "head shots" with the autographs of the stars. There's an entire industry in the collection and sale of these treasures. What I like about them is after the five and six-figure prices of so much memorabilia associated with Tinsel Town, you can easily pick up autographed head shots and promotional stills (photos released from the sets of movies and television shows) for under fifty dollars. From Ed Asner to Henry (the "Fonz") Winkler, from Lonni Anderson to Lindsay Wagner, you can collect quite a wall full without emptying your wallet.

True, signatures from superstars like Judy Garland will cost considerably more. To get hers on a scrap of paper will cost about $500; on a head shot, $1500; and on a photo of Judy as Dorothy, dig deep, *real* deep: $12,000. You're looking at similar costs for the stars of *Gone With the Wind*, with the exception of Hattie McDaniel, who as Mammy became the first African-American to win an Academy Award (Best Supporting Actress). Her signature is very rare, so just her autographs on a piece of paper costs about $1,000, and tops any of the marquee stars, including Garland.

One reason so many celebrity collectibles are so pricey is that the celebrities themselves often get into the act, sometimes in a big way. How Big? Let's look at Debbie Reynolds for a few moments. She's been a huge collector of Hollywood movie memorabilia, and was far-sighted enough to acquire thousands of props, costumes, and other items. She's now recognized as having the largest personally-owned collection in the world. It's valued at over $50 million and includes more than 3,500 costumes, including two that I've already mentioned: Marilyn Monroe's white dress – the one she's trying to hold down – in *The Seven Year Itch*, and Dorothy's slippers. A catalogue of Reynolds' collection once ran more than one-hundred fifty pages. That's quite a list.

Celebrities amass a lot more than costumes. That *National Treasure* Nicolas Cage was an enthusiastic collector of comic books. In fact, he took his stage name of Cage from his favorite comic book hero, Luke Cage. When his collection of one-hundred forty-one lots was auctioned by Heritage Auction House, it brought in a cool $1.68 million. How come it was worth so much? It included classics, like a 1940 Detective #38 Comic, which debuted Batman's sidekick, Robin; and a 1940 All-Star Comic #3, which was the first comic to introduce a superhero team, the Justice Society of America. And of course Cage's bounty contained the prized possession of every comic book collector: Action Comics #1, in which Superman made his first appearance.

Cage moved from comics to cars: Ferraris, Lamborghinis, Corvettes, and others, including a 1971 Lamborghini Miura VS. once owned by the Shah of Iran, who didn't prove nearly as durable – or as popular – as the car he once favored.

After considering Reynolds and Cage's obsessions, other celebrity collections strike a decidedly more populist profile. *The Price is Right's* Bob Barker collects military figurines and Bradford plates. He's acquired roughly one-hundred seventy-five of the latter. He's a big history buff, particularly military history. Maybe he should see if he can get on *Jeopardy*.

Billy Crystal is a big sports memorabilia collector. He actually went to Marshall University in Huntington, West Virginia on a baseball scholarship, but never played a game because the program was suspended his freshman year. Crystal's made up for that disappointment in two ways: he's collected a Mickey Mantle baseball glove and bat, and he signed a minor league baseball contract and played for one day for the New York Yanks during spring training. He wore uniform number 60, to mark his sixtieth birthday. How'd he do at the plate? Well, it's all relative, right? He fouled off a pitch, and was released the next day. Crystal also owns a boxing glove given to him by Muhammad Ali, and a basketball from Michael Jordan. It's nice to have friends in high places.

What about that crooner extraordinaire, the Chairman of the Board, Old' Blue Eyes himself? Sinatra collected trains. His Palm Springs home was filled with miniature trains, mostly Lionel and LGB. The Vatican gave him his most unusual item: an Italian wooden train. Frank's collection also included photographs of steam engines as well as framed paintings of trains.

Angelina Jolie collects knives (better behave yourself, Brad), Rosie O'Donnell collects McDonald's toys, and John Travolta has a love affair with aviation memorabilia. For Demi Moore, it's dolls and vintage clothing (nothing about boy toys that I could find). Jay Leno goes for motorcycles and automobiles. Patty Duke is all about Beanie Babies. Johnny Depp searches out insects and rare books, presumably not in the same places. Jamie Lee Curtis collects photographs. Celine Dion goes that extra mile to find c ollectible shoes.

Far more predictable are the collections of Dick Clark, the "World's Oldest Teenager," who has gathered together tons of rock 'n roll items (a lot more on rock 'n roll memorabilia in the next chapter); and Elvira, who searches out gothic goods. Her most unusual acquisition: A bat skeleton given to her by none other than Nicolas Cage, who might have admired her comic book qualities.

Now what about those celebrities who are only as real as our imaginations? Harry Potter and Winnie the Pooh were the two examples I mentioned at the start of this chapter. J.K. Rowling has sparked an entirely new river of collectibles that flow from everything from first editions to the original paintings for her book covers. Let's start at the start, with the British edition of her first Potter book, *Harry Potter and the Philosopher's Stone*. In appeared in 1997, and the original hardback, which was limited to a mere five-hundred copies, now sells for almost $40,000, if it's in fine condition. If this first edition has her signature, add another $10,000 to the value.

Philosopher's Stone is by far the most valuable of her first editions, but that's only because the book was such a sensation that her publisher started printing more hardcovers for all the others that followed in her inestimable series.

As for those original paintings depicting Potter and his world, the one by Thomas Taylor for *Philosopher's Stone* sold at auction for about $170,000. Again, subsequent cover art didn't go for as much, but Cliff Wright's painting for the *back* cover of *Chamber of Secrets* brought in $9,000, and an illustration of the flying Ford, Anglia, went for a cool $27,000.

Lest we veer too far away from movie props, a nineteenth century globe from *Philosopher's Stone* sold for about $35,000. And a crystal ball from the same movie pulled in about $2,500. A pair of Harry's wands in a special presentation box, originally given away at the movie premier and signed by Rowling, raised $23,000 for a cancer charity.

So J.K. Rowling has spawned quite a collecting fever around her young wizard, but she's a newbie compared to Winnie the Pooh. Now you might argue that Winnie *is* real. Unlike Potter, you can hold and hug the lovable critter. But clearly, he's not human, though his millions of fans might consider Winnie a superior species. He certainly holds his own among collectibles. As I noted earlier in this book, he's the world's most collectible bear, and he's held that title for decades.

As many of you know, Winnie sprang from the imagination of A. A. Milne, a prolific writer who died in 1956 at the age of seventy-three. While he saw great success for his "Bear of Little Brain," Winnie did not become a global, multimillion dollar industry until years after his death, when Disney began producing animated films of the cuddly creation, turbo charging interest in all things Winnie. That included substantial prices for a first edition pair of the books themselves: *Winnie the Pooh* and *House at Pooh Corner*, which sold at auction for approximately $11,000. *Pooh Lowers the Sail*, which are sketches by the illustrator Ernest Shepard, sold for nearly the same price. But they cost only a fraction of the $250,000 paid by the residents of Winnipeg, Canada, when they bought Shepard's only known oil painting of Winnie the Pooh.

The original Winnie, a bear in the London Zoo, was named after the city of Winnipeg, which explains the city's interest in the famous painting of the even more famous bear. The city hopes to drum up tourist trade for their fine prairie city, no doubt inspired by the intense interest in the Five Hundred Acre Wood near the village of Upper Hartfield, England. Ring a bell? It's the forest on which author Milne based his book *The Hundred Acre Wood*. In fact, the Poohsticks Bridge has born the weight of so many tourists that it had to undergo repairs not long ago. Interestingly enough, Milne's own home right nearby later became the residence of Brian Jones of the Rolling Stones. Shortly after Jones moved into the house, he drowned in the swimming pool.

It's only one of the many ways the worlds of literature, Hollywood, celebrities, and Rock 'n Roll comes together, usually far less tragically.

Time to review, shall we?

1) Props and costumes have long histories as collectibles.
2) Dorothy's slippers from *The Wizard of Oz* remain some of the most sought after Hollywood collectibles of all time.
3) The statue of the Maltese falcon is another iconic – and valuable – collectible.
4) Movie posters range in cost from under $10 to more than $450,000.
5) Signed "head shots" are consistently affordable.
6) Many celebrities are big collectors. Debbie Reynolds boasts the largest collection of props and costumes.

7) J.K. Rowling created a whole new realm of collectibles with her *Harry Potter* books.
8) After more than eighty years, Winnie the Pooh is still the top dog...er, bear.

Our enjoyable journey to celebrity collectibles has only begun. Why, we haven't even looked at the enormous and always growing interest in the notables of sports. But wait a second. Is that a sound check I'm hearing? It is indeed, and it's coming from...Chapter 8 – the world of rock 'n roll – where just about anything ever touched by a guitar hero has become a collectible.

Chapter 8
Peacock Jumpsuits and Psychedelic Limousines

Despite tabloid news reports to the contrary, it seems reasonable to conclude that the King of Rock 'n Roll, Elvis Presley, really did die on the fateful day of August 16, 1977. While his soul may have departed, he left behind an earthly kingdom of collectibles rivaled – but rarely surpassed – by only the highest order of rock's other royalty. Shall we start at the top of the charts, the Elvis price chart that is?

The single most expensive piece of Elvis memorabilia is his peacock jumpsuit, the one that he sported in performances. Recently, it told for $300,000, which broke the record for one of the King's classic cars, which had gone for $295,000. Compared to those figures, a veritable bargain could have been had for Elvis' jeweled cape at $105,250. A more accessible item (for the Elvis obsessed) might be one of his leather jackets for $37,000, or for his personal script for the film *Love Me Tender*: $5,400.

The value of all Elvis memorabilia just keeps on climbing, which often happens, as many of you know, when a super celebrity dies. Elvis left his stamp on virtually everything...just ask the U.S. Postal Service. The all-time most collected stamp – by a mammoth margin – is the one bearing Elvis Presley's youthful visage. That 29-cent stamp, issued in 1993, accounted for a whopping 124,000,000 stamps that were bought *but never used!* By the way, for you number crunchers, that calculates into almost $36 million income for the Postal Service.

Now nobody ever said collectors weren't ingenious. One of the best examples that I've run across, were the Presley collectors who took those stamps and mailed an envelope with a phony address, so the "letter" would be marked "Return to Sender." And if you're an Elvis fan, this immediately brings to mind the lyrics, "…address unknown????" (*Return to Sender* went to number two on the American Billboard singles chart in 1962. And those aptly marked envelopes have climbed in value, too.)

That stamp, if you bought it upon issue, was about as inexpensive as Elvis memorabilia is ever likely to get. But an Elvis movie or concert poster will usually break only a piggy bank, unless of course they're signed with Presley's inimitable flourish. As long as you stay within your budget, you're not likely to go wrong with the King. There are even Elvis-signed baseballs, though they're very tough to find. When you do come across one, be prepared to play hardball…for the hardball!

Thanks to Colonel Tom Parker, Elvis' longtime manager, there were any numbers of odd Elvis endorsements that have become seriously sought after collectibles. How odd? How about Elvis Presley Sneakers? No promises to jump higher or run faster, but purchasers who bought the sneakers, licensed by The King's combine in 1956, could get a green and black pair or a black and white pair. The green and black are the most valuable, though the sneakers in either color scheme are rare and worth upwards of $4,300, as long as they're in the tan box that they came in originally (always save the packaging, folks).

The Colonel – he was known by many names, not all of them printable – had Elvis on lipstick, cheap guitars, velvet paintings, hats, scarves, watches, you name it (a term never better applied than in this case.) But the Elvis endorsement I consider the most bizarre was for Elvis Presley Wine. Bizarre, because while Elvis reportedly had problems with prescription drugs – not enough to stop President Nixon from making him an honorary "Federal Agent-at-Large" in the then Bureau of Narcotics and Dangerous Drugs – Elvis rarely, if ever, consumed alcohol. And this was widely known. So how did the Colonel explain the endorsement? "Elvis never drank wine, but if he did, this is the wine he would have ordered." (The Colonel was a spin-meister before there were spin-meisters.)

By the way, the photograph of Elvis and President Nixon from their Oval Office *tête-à-tête* is a huge collectible, though not a particularly valuable one. How could that be? It's the single most requested photograph from the eight million photos in the National Archives, beating out Buzz Aldrin walking on the moon, the American flag rising on Iwo Jima, or any other truly iconic photograph, including the thousands of snaps taken of American presidents and dignitaries. If you want a copy for yourself, just contact the Archives (www.archives.gov/research/formats/photos.html).

Regardless of how you feel about Elvis as an entertainer, he is rock's original Bigfoot, which is why his collectibles are so darn...collectible. As the years go by, it's easy to lose track of just how huge a phenomenon Elvis was. Let's look at just a few numbers. Industry experts estimate he's sold more than one *billion* record units worldwide – more than anyone in history. He had one-hundred forty-nine songs on Billboards' Hot 100 Pop Chart, eighteen of which went to number one. And he had scores of hits on the country and western, rhythm and blues, and gospel charts. He also starred in thirty-one feature films and two concert documentaries.

In October, 2005, Variety Magazine inducted him into their top ten entertainment icons of the twentieth century, along with the Beatles, Marilyn Monroe, Lucille Ball, Marlon Brando, Humphrey Bogart, Louis Armstrong, Charlie Chaplin, James Dean, and Mickey Mouse. It's no surprise, naturally, that the collectibles of that top ten also rank as among the most valuable in the world.

Another reason Presley memorabilia, along with the collectibles of all those other immensely famous faces, is likely to gain value in the long run is that memorabilia is mortal, just like the outsized personality who gave value to his flamboyant capes and flashy cars. A stark – some might say tragic – example of this occurred in 2007, when Castle Kashan in Malibu was destroyed by one of California's nastier wildfires. The blaze destroyed a priceless collection of The King's treasures. About the only items saved were Elvis' Army fatigues and thirty-two films scripts with his handwritten margin notes. Everything else went up in smoke (No, we're not segueing to Creech and Chong here, though those two *dube*-ious celebs of vinyl and celluloid have lots of memorabilia, too; some of it's even legal.)

A contemporary of Elvis' early success in the 1950s was Buddy Holly. When his items went up for auction a few years ago, the results proved staggering. The collectible that drew the most attention was Buddy's 14-karat white gold wristwatch for $155,350. The provenance of that watch played a role in turbo charging its value: Buddy Holly was wearing it when the plane he was on crashed outside of Clear Lake, Iowa on February 3, 1959. Of course, all you music buffs know that that day was immortalized in Don McLean's *American Pie* ballad as "...the day the music died." Richie Valens also died in the crash. In the same auction, Holly's passport went for $26,290.

Recent auctions have also seen The Beach Boys' articles of incorporation from 1964 go for $22,750, and a sealed copy of the Beatles' gruesome *Butcher* cover album (quickly withdrawn amid a hullaballoo and re-released with a much more staid appearance) in its original shrink-wrap snagged $38, 387.

The Beatles are truly an entity unto themselves in rock 'n roll memorabilia, dwarfing, in some respects, even The King. John Lennon alone dominates the top five rock 'n roll collectibles, based on dollar value alone.

1) **John Lennon's Rolls-Royce Phantom V limousine,** with psychedelic paintwork: **$2.6 million.**

2) **Lennon's Steinway Model "Z" piano** that he used to compose *Imagine:* **$2.1 million.** The upright came with Lennon's cigarette burns. Pop star George Michael bought it, and then turned the venerable piano over to the Beatles Story museum in Liverpool.

3) **Jerry Garcia's "Tiger" guitar** for almost **$1 million.**

4) **Jerry Garcia's "Wolf" guitar** for almost **$800,000.** It sold at auction the same day that "Tiger" went up on the block.

5) **Eric Clapton's "Brownie" guitar,** used to record *Layla,* went for almost **$315,000** at Christie's.

"Get back...JoJo..." to the Beatles. Specifically, to Lennon because the Fab Four are not equals in the world of collectibles. At one time the pecking order was John, Paul, George, and Ringo. But since his death, George has moved into the number two slot. Lennon still rules, though, and Ringo still rides the caboose. But let's put the famous drummer into perspective: he still ranks near the top relative to other rockers.

What's considered really hot in Beatles memorabilia? Anything with all four of the lads' signatures. One expert says he's seen only one *White Album* signed by all of them, and that he's never run across an *Abbey Road* or *Let It Be* album bearing autographs from the entire group.

As with most rockers, there's a huge variety of Beatles' collectibles available. You can indulge in videos, lasers, DVDs, concert tickets, Beatles comic books, artwork, a Lennon whiskey decanter ($150-$200, shades of Colonel Tom Parker),

Beatles candy, Beatles bubble gum "records," Apple Records matches (green), tickets to a Lennon/Yoko Ono Christmas party at Royal Albert Hall, among thousands of items.

What may grab many fans the most, though (certainly the ones who can't afford to plop down a couple of mil for a limousine) may be music related items, such as the picture sleeve for the single for *Girl/You're Going To Lose That Girl*. Some of you may already be nodding your heads, knowing why it's a collectible: at the last moment the label withdrew the 45 as a single. The sleeve has been available for $20. Another picture sleeve, which includes the promotional copy of *Please Me/From Me To You* is much pricier at $2,500. But that's nothing compared to *A Hard Day's Night* on pink vinyl – a one of a kind – for $10,000.

So it's easy to see how you could focus just on Elvis or the Beatles, and then narrow your aim even more by collecting just their concert tickets or posters or 45s. *Beatology Magazine* is worth checking out if you decide to collect Beatles memorabilia. There are also official price guides to Beatles records and memorabilia, as there are for Elvis' as well.

That piano of Lennon's was a monster sale, and intriguing in that it holds second place in the most valued of all rock collectibles. Intriguing because, let's face it, guitars are the instrument that gave rock its roll. Which is not to say that guitars aren't hot items, because they certainly are, witness Clapton and Garcia nipping at Lennon's heels on that top five list?

Guitars owned and played by rock's wunderkinds almost always fetch a pretty penny. One of Kurt Cobain's recently sold for $131,450. But just as Hollywood memorabilia was dominated by a single star, Debbie Reynolds, the collection of guitars has long been ruled by Randy Bachman of *Bachman Turner Overdrive* and *The Guess Who*. Bachman collected more than three-hundred seventy-five Gretsch guitars – reputed to be the finest collection of Gretsch electric guitars in the world. Bachman recently sold his collection to the Gretsch Company for its museum. The worth of Randy's collection; several million dollars, according to accounts quoting the rocker. The collection also includes Gretsch amplifiers, banjos, Dobos, ukuleles, and an organ.

But even a member of rock's royal court can't count on getting every guitar that he wants. For more than thirty years, Bachman has been trying to recover a late 1950s orange Gretsch guitar. It's the Chet Atkins model, stolen in 1976 from Bachman's hotel room. Bachman considers the instrument his first real professional guitar, and he played it on what is arguably BTO's biggest hit *Takin' Care of Business.*

Alas, he's never recovered the guitar, so this is one bit of business that Bachman is still trying to take care of. Meantime, after hearing of Bachman's loss, the ever amiable Chet Atkins sent Randy a guitar similar to the one that had been stolen, replete with an autographed pick-guard. This guitar is quite a collectible, too. There are only three of them. Chet owns one. So does that genial fellow, Paul McCartney, and now Bachman, who did not sell Chet's gift to the Gretsch guitar company.

Further down the guitar food chain, you'll find an Eric Clapton signed guitar for $6,000 (we already know what a *Clapton* owned guitar can cost), a Peter Townsend played six-string for $3,800, a Stevie Nicks tambourine for $1,300 (I can feel myself reaching for the silk scarves already), and Phil Collins drumsticks for $1,200.

Here's a quick list of some of the more valuable signed album covers:

The Beatles – *Meet the Beatles* - $7,500 (signed by all the members)

Bob Dylan – *The Times They Are A Changin'* - $1,800

Michael Jackson – *Thriller* - $800

Elton John – *Captain Fantastic and The Brown Dirt Cowboy* - $850

Janis Joplin – *Big Brother* - $1,900

Madonna – *I'm Breathless* - $600

Metallica – *And Justice For All* - $1,600

Stevie Nicks – *Rumours* - $800
Pink Floyd – *The Wall* - $850
Elvis Presley – *Love Me Tender* - $3,100
Prince – *Around the World In A Day* - $750
Queen – *A Night At The Opera*- $1,900
Otis Redding – *The Soul Album* - $800
The Rolling Stones – *Five By Five* - $1,700
Bruce Springsteen – *Lucky Town* - $650
The Yardbirds – *Over Under Sideways Down* - $1,400

The following are approximate values for the clothing and accessories of rock's biggest stars:

John Lennon – Eyeglasses: $30,000 -$40.000.
James Brown – Stage outfit: $12,000.
Alice Cooper – Devil costume: $3,500.
Mick Jagger – Silk tie: $1,000.
Elton John – Stage-worn suit: $5,000.
Jack Wilson – Black overcoat: $600.
Diana Ross – Stage-worn dresses: $1,500.
Prince – Complete stage outfit, including, coat, trousers, handkerchief,
 and boots: $24,000.
Keith Richards – Felt fedora with matching silk hat band: $2,500.
MC Hammer – Baseball-style jacket: $650.
George Michael – Black leather biker jacket: $4,000.
Roy Orbison – Western-style cream suit: $2,500.
Phil Collins – Cream-colored double-breasted stage suit: $1,800.
Elvis Costello – Stage jacket: $1,950.
Paula Abdul – State-worn shirt: $250.
Cher – Brown leather bomber jacket: $1,000.
Eric Clapton – Turquoise leather stage shoes: $2,700.
Marvin Gaye – Brown velvet stage jacket: $2,100.

It pays to keep in mind that the value of clothing, and accessories like eyeglasses, will almost always increase, especially if there are new releases, or re-releases, from the entertainer. But make sure you store the clothing carefully. You don'l want Clapton's turquoise stage shoes to fade from direct sunlight. And in case you're wondering, the answer is yes: some collectors do try on the celebrity clothing that they've bought. When I obtained a George Harrison Nehru jacket, I not only tried it on, so did everyone in my office. Just don't go trying to pack ten pounds of potatoes into a five-pound bag, if you know what I mean. We don't want those seams splitting. Also, make sure you get an LOA, a letter of authenticity that verifies the clothing's provenance.

By now, you might have had repeated bouts of sticker shock. Lots of rock memorabilia *is* pricey, but not all of it, and I'm not just talking about the Elvis offering by the U.S. Postal Service. Concert programs are highly collectible and eminently affordable. Try one from a Blondie concert In 1979 for $40 (all values approximate). Or Springsteen in 1981 for $60. A concert program for Oscar winner Melissa Etheridge comes in at around $35. Of course, if you want the program for the granddaddy of them all, Woodstock 1969, you'll have to fork out about $500. And these are all unsigned, mind you.

But rock, like Hollywood, loves signed photos. You can have one of Jimmy Page from *Led Zeppelin for $230*, Simon and Garfunkel's for $250, Cheech and Chong for $100 or a Carly signed photographs for $130. There are scores of signed photographs available.

Also highly desirable – and reasonable – is signed sheet music. Again, I'll offer only a sampling: Jerry Lee Lewis' *Great Balls of Fire, $250;* Fats Domino's *Blueberry Hill, $230;* and Sting's *Fields of Gold, $150.*

Backstage passes, so sought after at shows, come in at much more reasonable prices. You could pick one up for U2's 1985, *The Unforgettable Fire tour for $40.* Or spend $30 for a Bob Seeger's "Artist Guest" pass from 1983. Sweet Baby James Taylor's backstage pass for his *Pull Over* tour in 2001 can be had for under $20. The same amount of cash can nab a pass for The Cranberries '94/95 world tour. I strongly suspect that many backstage passes are among the very few rock collectibles that actually decrease in value in the weeks and years after a show. What am I saying? That' I've known of frantic fans willing to spend a great deal to get backstage on the night of a concert, when cash isn't the only currency (hence, the popularity of the term "sex, drugs, and rock and roll").

You'll find that guitar picks are usually modestly priced. Picks for all of the following can be had for under $50: Van Helen, Santana, Eagles, Arlo Guthrie, John Oates, and Dave Matthews. You can buy picks for many other bands and individual artists in the same price range.

Vintage concert tickets cover a wide range of prices. A Janis Joplin ticket to the Swing Auditorium in San Bernardino, California in 1969 will run you about $325. Sly and the Family Stone from 1973 costs only $45. Eagles from 1980: $40. Doobie Brothers from 1975: $55. And, Joni Mitchell from 1976: $40.

In a class of its own is a three-day ticket for Woodstock 1969. That goes for about $300. You could specialize on Woodstock alone and have plenty of items to keep you busy. Start with the ticket and move on to Life Magazine's Special Edition *Woodstock Musical Festival* in September 1969, priced at $150. *Rolling Stone's* U.K. Woodstock issue is available for a few dollars more at $170. The same price could get you the original Woodstock Movie Program. Or you could start collecting contracts of the bands that played there. *The Who's* contract is available – and I can scarcely believe this – for $15 (I think I'm going to pick that one up.)

The truth is I won't snatch up that contract, but when you start researching collectibles, you will find yourself astonished at times at the bargains. I say, *trust your gut.* If you think something's a steal, it might be. Or it might indicate that in future years there could be value in the investment.

I'd strongly urge anyone looking into rock 'n roll collectibles to spend time surfing the Net. There are lots of websites with lots of stories, because that's what collecting is all about – the stories. Not just the ones behind the item, but the stories that explain how you found a particular collectible. The items we collect are many things to many people, but to almost all of us they are conversation pieces of the first order.

Here's our review of rock 'n roll collectibles.

1) Elvis memorabilia covers every aspect of his career: rock 'n roll, films, along with scores of endorsements for questionable –but highly collectible – products.

2) Elvis meeting with President Nixon in the White House is the most requested photo in the entire National Archives.

3) Elvis and the Beatles are rock's only members of *Variety Magazine's* top ten entertainment icons of the twentieth century.

4) John Lennon's limousine and upright piano rank number one and two in the list of rock's most valuable memorabilia

5) Randy Bachman of *BTO* and *The Guess Who* recently sold the world's largest and finest collection of Gretsch electric guitars to a museum owned by the company that made them.

6) Some of rock's most highly sought after collectibles are album covers, clothing, and accessories.

7) More modestly priced are classic concert programs, signed photos, signed sheet music, backstage passes, guitar picks, and vintage concert tickets.

On that note (pun intended), it's time to get really warmed up, loosen those muscles, and continue our enjoyable journey to the third of the big three collectibles for an overview of sports memorabilia.

Action Comics #1: First Appearance of Superman June, 1938

Signed Lithograph of the Greatest NBA Players 1946-1996

Fab Four figurines from the early 1960's.

Basketball star Bob Pettit's size 20 shoes

Rare picture and signed ball from midget Eddie Gaedel

A signed-worn hat from the Chairman of the Board, Frank Sinatra

A rare pair of the Kissing Kennedys' bobblehead dolls

First copies of <u>People</u>, <u>Playboy</u> and <u>Mad</u> magazines

Program and boxing glove of Muhammed Ali, aka "Cassius Clay"

Original sheet music from various Presidential Campaigns

Gramophone and dog "Nipper"

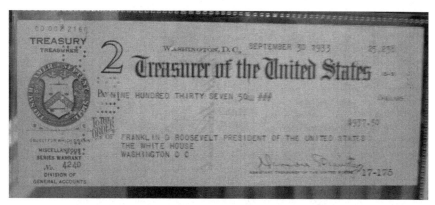

Actual payroll check made out and endorsed by Franklin D. Roosevelt

Game-worn Jersey of Sandy Koufax

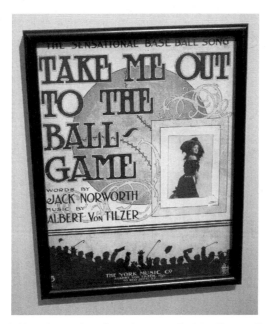

Original Sheet Music of "Take Me Out to the Ballgame"

Items of the <u>Teddy Bears.</u> The author's cousin is on the left.

A signed envelope signed by the president who served
the shortest time in office, William Henry Harrison.

A rare 'Holy Grail' baseball card of Honus Wagner.

All pictures are courtesy of the Figler Foundation Museum

Chapter 9
The Rising Value of Sports Memorabilia

Twenty years ago, if someone had predicted that a golfer would become *numero uno* in the world of sports collectibles – an African-American golfer at that – there would have been a lot of skepticism. African-Americans hadn't dominated the game, and golf itself had always held narrow appeal, unlike baseball, basketball, and football. A *duffer?* Come on, watcha talkin'?

But that's exactly what happened with the meteoric rise of Tiger Woods. To call him a superstar in the world of collectibles does no more justice to his stature among auction houses than to say that "one of a kind" accurately assesses his legacy on the links. Tiger Woods transcends sports, so much so that if you could collect his sneezes, they'd probably be worth a bundle, too.

But Woods also demonstrates the volatility of values in the world of memorabilia. After his wife put a golf club through his car window, and his nickname "Sultan of Swing" became a double entendre, the value of his collectibles took a dip.

Here's a for instance: The golf ball that Woods sank to win the Masters in 2005 was worth an estimated $100,000. After the scandal heard round the world? About $10,000.

Now those are estimates, guesses really, because the owner of that particular golf ball isn't actually testing the waters. But Tiger's memorabilia is still bankable, and likely to rebound. Why? It's that old law of supply and demand. Woods has always been known as a "tough autograph." He's never been fast and loose with his John Hancock (maybe with other aspects of his personal life, but not with his signature), so there's a strong likelihood that Woods' collectibles will regain their former platinum status. Meantime, hold on to whatever you've got and sit tight. And if you see a good buy on a Woods' item, I'd say snap it up. The only superstar in sports whose values ever remained low after a scandal was O.J. Simpson, and that's an infinitely less savory story. And if you can get your hands on the club that went through the window, that would constitute a Woods' collectible of the first order.

Like Tiger Woods, the classic film *Field of Dreams* possesses its own kind of resilience in the world of memorabilia. It's Hollywood magic, but it's about a treasured national institution – baseball. In this case, combining baseball and the big screen has spawned cross-pollinating collectibles of the first order.

But it wouldn't have happened if the filmmakers hadn't come up with an outstanding story: Farmer Ray Kinsella builds a baseball field after hearing a voice say "If you build it, he will come." That ball field became larger than life on celluloid, and now occupies a hallowed place in our memories...and in our memorabilia.

Now this is what I love – and why I make a point of mentioning *Field of Dreams*: the mythical diamond has spawned some very real associations with the biggest names in baseball. A poster for the film, signed by Mickey Mantle, Ted Williams, and Joe DiMaggio sold recently for almost $8,000. A *poster.* But a poster signed by the film's star, Kevin Costner, was valued at "only" $500, proving the point: cross-pollination *is* potent.

You can immerse yourself in this kind of *Field of Dreams' memorabilia,* but you can do more than that: you can stand on the field itself. The baseball diamond that was built for the film, based upon a fictional character's fantasy, has now become a very real tourist attraction, rich with the lore of the game, real *and* imagined. Wrap your head around that one.

The world from which the film arose was the era of the most notable player in the history of baseball memorabilia, Honus Wagner. Remember Honus from the introduction to this book? Time to give him some serious face time.

To ardent baseball fans, Wagner rings a huge bell; but if your knowledge of baseball is confined to other household names like Ruth, DiMaggio, and Mantle, remember that Honus was one of the first five players inducted into the Hall of Fame, right behind Ty Cobb, and tied with Ruth. One of the true celestials.

But why is a simple baseball card with his picture on it far and away the most valuable sports card in history? That's a story with a murky, mysterious beginning.

As I mentioned in the introduction, the American Tobacco Company issued the T206 set of baseball cards from 1909 to 1911. The cards came with two brands of cigarette boxes, Sweet Caporal and Piedmont. At that time, the cigarette companies were the ones promoting their products with cards; bubble gum and cereal companies hadn't gotten in on the act yet.

Now legend would have you believe that Wagner demanded the American Tobacco Company stop printing his card as soon as he learned that his face was being used to sell cigarettes. And that may be true. But there is some controversy on this point for two reasons: first, Wagner smoked; and second, perhaps more important, it's said that Wagner wanted more money than the twenty bucks players were getting paid for the rights to use their faces. That wouldn't have been much recompense to a prince of the baseball diamond like Wagner.

Regardless of the reason, Wagner *did* put a stop to the use of his photo on those cards, and the result was that few Wagner cards were issued; only twenty to thirty of them are thought to exist today. Okay, it's possible, *always* possible, that a few more might show up from the back of some-body's grandfather's shed, but most experts consider that unlikely because, among collectors, it's been long known that this is a card from which complete retirement funds can be made.

Because baseball cards have been so avidly collected – and their values carefully recorded – we can chart the rise of the Wagner card from some very humble beginnings.

1940 – The Wagner card listed in a price guide for $2.50.
1945 – The card jumps to $25 in value.
1960 – Wagner doubles in value to $50.
1971 – Honus' card doubles again to $100.

And then the story of the cards' value takes off like the first space mission. In the baseball card-collecting craze that mushroomed in the 1980s, the Wagner card leaped in value to $100,000, depending on the condition (of course). Can you imagine if you'd bought that baby for a hundred smackeroos in 1971? But the story, I mean the card – no, I mean both the story *and* the card– gets richer. In the 1990s, a certain hockey player named Wayne Gretzky and Los Angeles Kings owner Bruce McNall paid $451,000 for a Wagner card (henceforth, that particular Wagner card would be known as the Gretzky card.)

Wal-Mart bought the Gretzky card in 1996 for a promo-tion, which was won by a Florida woman who put it up for auction. It fetched $640,500. The Gretzky later sold to a

California man for $1.1 million. The last time it sold it went for $2.8 million.

Not all the Wagner cards are worth that much, but they're all considered to be real prizes. So by all means cast your eyes on those long neglected boxes in attics and basements. And if you do find an old collection covered with a lifetime's dust, you just might receive the shock – and thrill – of a lifetime by finding a new Honus Wagner card. It's every collector's dream, and it does happen. But before you spend any money, have it graded by an expert to make sure it's not a counterfeit, and that it's one of the higher quality Wagners.

For more about the Wagner card and the controversies it has generated, you might want to read the book *The Card* by Michael O'Keefe and Teri Thompson.

That baseball card-collecting craze I just referred to was amazing, and for high-end cards like the Wagner, it remains strong. But it's a very different story for the baseball card industry overall. In 1991, the industry set a record $1.1 billion in sales and by 2005, that figure had dropped to $300 million. Predictably, the number of card shops around the country fell (almost proportionately), from about 4,500 to 1,200. Keep in mind that the primary sport in the card industry – and with the card shops – is baseball.

So what happened? For starters, there was a glut of cards that appeared in the 1980s and 1990s. Trading cards had become such big business that more and more card manufacturers tried to cash in. At one point, there were *eighty* companies churning out trading cards. When you keep in mind that the biggest business of cards is baseball, you also have to look at what's happened to the popularity of the game over the past two decades. Simply put, baseball is not as preeminently popular as it once was. Blame it on the steroid scandals, labor strikes, or the surge in popularity of football, basketball, and auto racing. All of those factors played a role in baseball's decline.

Am I predicting baseball's ultimate demise? Absolutely not. I think it's a great game, but it has to compete with a lot of serious competition for the entertainment dollar, and not all of the competitors come from the realm of sports. Just look at electronic games, which now surpass movies in the amount of money consumers spend on them. That's a very different situation from twenty plus years ago; just something for the prudent collector to keep in mind.

Also keep in mind that even with some fall-off, trading cards remain one of the most popular form of collectibles, so if you're drawn to them, here are some pointers.

Start by looking at the modern era of baseball cards, which begins after World War II. If you're just getting going, in all likelihood this is the era that will grab your attention, and which remains somewhat affordable (at least you won't be looking at six and seven-figure prices.)

Keep in mind that the top five companies of the modern era are Topps, Fleer, Score, Upper Deck, and Dunress (formerly Leaf, Dunruss is now owned by the Panini Group).

By way of background, Topps started issuing baseball cards in 1951 and after buying out a lesser name competitor became the only company issuing major league baseball cards sets from 1956 to 1980. Topps proved amazingly successful in signing virtually every major league player to an exclusive contract, and only companies promoting products such as cereal, meats, and soda fell outside the exclusive Topps agreement. A court ruled in 1980 and 1981 that Fleer and Donruss could issue cards, but not with gum. (By the way, do you know why bubble gum is pink? I love this story. When a Fleer employee invented the gum in 1928, the only food coloring at the plant was pink. The name of the gum? My favorite: Double Bubble.)

So Fleer's been producing cards for a long time. They've also put out cards of movie stars, The Three Stooges, Hogan's Heroes, along with football and basketball cards.

Donruss got into the act in 1958, turning out cards based on television shows and musical groups. In 1981, the company issued its first set of baseball cards.

Upper Deck started even later, in 1989. Its cards are unique because the company included a hologram on the back of each card as a deterrent to counterfeiters. Their cards cost more than the competition, but they've been very popular with collectors.

Those are the big five, with Topps still...*tops*. For the newbie card collector, I can suggest several ways to build a collection

1) Collect by player. Try to acquire as many cards of Craig Biggio or Wayne Causey as you can, for example.
2) Collect by team.
3) Collect by other criteria, such as no-hit pitchers, Hall of Famers, or pitchers who have won twenty games in a season. There are reams of possibilities for the creative collector.

Here are the main factors that determine a card's value:

1) Rarity of the card.
2) If the card is the rookie card of the player.
3) If the player is a star, or better yet a Hall of Famer.

Cards are rated based on their condition. There are six card grades:

1) **Mint.** A mint card is perfect and has no damage. Well-centered, sharp corners and the picture is glossy.
2) **Excellent.** An excellent card is an almost perfect card. The corners are still sharp, there are no creases, and the gloss shows only a little wear. There is no visible damage at all, but the card may be a little off-center.

3) **Very good.** A very good card probably has a little damage (from handling), but there are no major creases. The corners aren't as sharp as a mint or excellent card, and may show some rounding. A very good card is an ideal card for collectors who want to keep their costs down but still have a nice collection.

4) **Good.** A good card does show an amount of wear not seen on higher-graded cards. There may be creases or a bit of rounding. In general, there are some visible problems.

5) **Fair.** A fair card displays quite a lot of damage, such as slight tearing, pen or pencil marks, pin or staple holes, and large or multiple creases. The card is still together, and is still valuable if it is a rare card.

6) **Poor.** A poor card may have water damage, large holes, parts that may be torn off, back damage because of glue or tape removal, and possibly major pen or pencil writing.

If you decide to collect cards, and millions of people have, pick up a couple of very good books on the subject: *300 Great Baseball Cards of the 20th Century* by Mike Piney, and *The Standard Catalog of Baseball Cards* published by Krause Publications.

Naturally, there's a lot more to sports memorabilia than cards. For all sports you can collect balls, jerseys, caps, gloves, bats, kicking tees, hockey sticks, shoes, uniforms, programs, tickets, bobbleheads, videos, board games, books, and many other ancillary items.

There are also sports memorabilia mysteries real enough to bring out the Sherlock Holmes in each of us. Mysteries, I should add, that if they're ever solved will bring a huge paycheck to the successful sleuth.

One of my favorites concerns "The Shot Heard 'Round the World," New York Giants' Bobby Thomson's homerun to beat the Brooklyn Dodgers in the 1951 National League playoff. No one knows with absolute certainty what happened to that ball, but for many years a gentleman named Bill Moore claimed that he owned it. He had a sweet story to back him up, too. Basically, that a childless friend of his father's scooped up the ball after it cleared the left field fence at the Polo Grounds and gave it to Moore's father for little Billy. Good enough for one affluent collector, who ponied up $47,824 for it. But if the ball were actually verified as *the* ball with which Bobby Thomson ended Dodger dreams? Now that would be worth at least a million big ones. Will it ever be known for sure? That's the mystery.

Here's another top-ranked mystery, and how it was solved. Jerry Kramer was a right guard on the Green Bay Packers when they defeated the Kansas City Chiefs in the first AFL-NFL Championship game in 1967. (This was even before they called it the Super Bowl.) Kramer was given a championship ring, which is a highlight for most pro football players.

However, in 1981, fourteen years later, Kramer was on a United Airlines flight from Chicago to New York. He took off the ring in the restroom to wash his hands, left it on the countertop (ouch!), and returned to his seat. Then he realized what he'd done and scooted back to the...scene of the crime...because that's what the lavatory had become: the ring had been stolen.

Flight attendants and the pilots pleaded for whoever took it to return the ring. No one did.

Kramer thought the ring was gone for good. Aha, but then he received a mysterious phone call from a person in Canada asking if he was missing his Super Bowl ring (by now it was called the Super Bowl). Kramer confirmed the loss. The guy hung up. But then the phone rang again, and this time Kramer learned that the ring was being auctioned.

Kramer called the auction company and told them that the ring had been stolen. Bids for the ring had already topped $20,000, but the company withdrew the ring from its offerings. Kramer now has his ring back. But what happened to that ring for fourteen years remains a mystery.

As one of the three big sports, football memorabilia can command hefty sums. Franco Harris, the first African-American – and Italian-American – to be named a Super Bowl MVP (the Steelers won four Super Bowls in the 1970s with Harris in the backfield) saw one of his football jerseys sell for just shy of $27,000. Franco, who owns a bakery in "The City of Steel," might have called that a lot of "dough" (sorry, couldn't resist) for a jersey he used to shed as casually as he did tacklers.

Another jersey – worn by Roger Maris when he hit his record 61st home run – sold for $302,000, considerably more than the estimated worth of the ball itself, which is now in the $50,000 to $60,000 range.

Baseballs are charming collectibles, though. I have a few myself, and I can tell you from personal experience that people are tantalized by seeing balls that have traveled over time to live large in our imaginations. Here are some tips if you're thinking about collecting baseballs, or you've already started. I'll begin with possible categories.

1) Single-signed balls. Like ones signed by Roberto Clemente.
2) Team signed balls.
3) All-Star game balls.
4) Historical balls, like one from the last game ever played at the Polo Grounds.
5) Milestone balls. A good example would be balls from the only players to ever throw perfect games.
6) Celebrity balls. We've talked about them – balls signed by rockers and movie stars.

It's best to collect autographs on official Major League baseballs, or if they're older on an American or National League ball. But don't look a gift horse in the mouth. Say you're strolling through a sporting goods store and you spot Alex Rodriquez, snag whatever ball you can get and get him to sign it, preferably with a Sharpie pen on the "sweet spot," which is the white space centered on the shortest distance between the two seams on the ball (in the event you've grabbed a baseball.)

Let yourself get creative if you collect baseballs. You could come up with a category no one's ever thought of. It might even prove profitable.

Now here are some "do nots" when collecting baseballs:

1) Do not handle the ball too often.
2) Do not retrace over a faded signature.
3) Do not display a baseball in direct sunlight.
4) Do not try to preserve a ball by adding a substance to its surface.
5) Do not keep the balls in a wet or poorly ventilated area.

Just as with baseball cards, there are factors that affect the value of a ball.

1) Type of ball. An "official" ball is preferred.
2) Legibility. Some players have meticulous signatures, other do not (Greg Maddux is a good example of the latter).
3) Placement of the signature. With single-signed balls, remember the "sweet spot."
4) Scarcity and demand. Some players sign a lot, others do not.
5) Condition of the ball. Is it a new ball or a beat-up one? If it is beat-up, is it a game-used ball, which would be preferred.
6) Completeness of the signatures. Did the player, for instance, sign Joe S. or Joe Smith?

If you do collect single-signed baseballs, you won't go wrong with balls signed by Babe Ruth, Lou Gehrig, Mickey Mantle, Mel Ott, Jackie Robinson, Roberto Clemente, Ted Williams, or Joe DiMaggio.

Just take a look at some very recent Tiger Woods memorabilia sales. A single signed *baseball* by Woods sold for almost $6,000 recently. That really is incredible. You can pick up signed baseballs by major stars for a hundred bucks. Rock performers, including Clapton, Dylan, the Rolling Stones, and the Beatles have all signed baseballs. So have Abbott and Costello, Frank Sinatra, Humphrey Bogart, Bob Hope, George Burns, and every president since William Howard Taft, but none of those balls come even close to the value of the one signed by Tiger Woods.

In another recent auction, a 1998 "Champions of Golf" Tiger Woods card in mint condition sold for just over $2,700. That was for an *unsigned* card. Those kinds of prices are usually reserved for either a signed card or a vintage card from at least fifty years ago. The "Champions of Golf" card was only ten years old. Two words describe this phenomenon: *unheard of.* We're talking about a young man in his early thirties, who's expected to become the world's first billionaire athlete any day now.

Remember that old Waylon and Willie song *Mamas Don't Let Your Babies Grow Up to be Cowboys?* Heck no, not if there's a golf club around. That pretty much sums up Tiger's back story. At age two, he putted against Bob Hope on *The Mike Douglas Show,* and at age three he shot a forty-eight in nine holes. The kid was even featured in Golf Digest at age five, and on ABC's *That's Incredible.* What has he achieved as an adult?

I'll summarize because otherwise it would take too long. He's won fourteen major golf championships, and sixty-six Professional Golf Association Tour events, which places him third on the all-time list. (Remember, he's a young man). He's got more major career wins and career PGA Tour wins than any other golfer out there today. He's also the youngest player to pull off the career Grand Slam. And I should add that he's the youngest golfer to win fifty tournaments on the tour. He's been PGA Player of the Year a record nine times and the Associated Press Male Athlete of the Year four times, which ties a record. The accomplishments – and accolades – just don't stop for quite a while, but I will. If you're among the uninitiated, I'm sure you get the picture. And if you know about Tiger, none of this is new.

Tiger transcends sports. I'm often asked if there are any "no brainers" in sports collectibles. At the very top of my list is any Tiger Woods item. Better yet, if you have a Woods collectible, keep it in a vault. Well, I'm only kidding about that, but you really do have memorabilia of real value. Yes, Wood's off the course activities have definitely tarnished his reputation and the value of his memorabilia has suffered, however, his popularity is still very high.

Figurines are another popular sport collectible. The company that that really put them on the map was Hartland Plastics of Milwaukee, Wisconsin. From 1958 to 1962, Hartland issued a set of baseball figurines that depicted eighteen renowned players, nine each from the American and National Leagues. They sold for $1.98. Depending on their condition, which is always the great caveat with collectibles, they're now worth about $300. Having the box and/or tag that they came in will increase the value (as always.)

But don't get fooled by a 25th anniversary set issued by Hartland about twenty years ago. The values of those figurines are only a fraction of the originals.

Hartland also issued a series depicting football players, including Johnny Unitas. But interestingly enough, collectors consider the most valuable pieces to be the depictions of Louisiana State University players of that era.

If the Hartland statues are too rich for your blood, let me give you a tip: think about collecting McFarlane Sports Figurines. Todd McFarlane, some of you may know, was the man who paid $3.1 million for the ball that Mark McGuire hit for his 70th homerun a few years ago. McFarlane's sports figurines are hot items and well worth collecting. He stared producing them in 2000. The figures are amazingly detailed, and the company has been careful not to saturate the market with too many of the figures, adding only twenty to thirty new players each year. They generally retail for $10 to $15. I think the McFarlane statues will be around for some time. Just a thought.

I'll have a whole chapter on the future of collectibles a little later. Right now, it's time to sum up, but before doing so I just want to say that if you feel your preferred sport has been slighted, please forgive me. The world of sports memorabilia is huge, and what I've tried to do is offer you a primer in this chapter, using principles of collecting that you can apply to just about any sport.

All right, let's review.

1) Tiger Woods demonstrates the ups and downs of memorabilia after a scandal, but the scarcity of his collectibles makes it likely that his collectibles will retain their rarefied values.
2) *Field of Dreams'* combination of Hollywood and sports has produced valuable memorabilia.
3) Honus Wagner is the MVP of all baseball collectibles.
4) Baseball card collecting, despite a downturn, remains one of the most popular of all activities for collectors.
5) Sports memorabilia has led to mysteries that have yet to be solved.
6) Collecting baseballs is immensely popular.
7) Sports figurines have been collected avidly for more than half a century.

Our joyful journey will continue with a most unusual superstar. His name is John Brey, and he reigns *numero uno* in the crazy and competitive world of Bobbleheads.

Chapter 10
King of the Bobbleheads

I've had the pleasure of meeting the King of the Bobbleheads, and I think you should, too. His name is John Brey, a transplanted New Jerseyan who moved to Florida for the good life...and found it with Bobbleheads. His experience with those cute, whacky looking dolls embodies everything I said in my introduction about the popularity of collectibles. Say what? Let me explain.

John's Bobbleheads make him feel a strong connection to his childhood, and they're a quality product much different from contemporary Bobbleheads. Moreover, his chosen collectible has made him a pile of money. And most important, John Brey, King of the Bobbleheads, has a lot of fun. Or as the King himself puts it, "It's the best job in the world."

Okay, first things first. You might be thinking, "What the heck is a Bobblehead?" You've seen them, trust me. Maybe when you were a kid you went to the ball park to watch the Yankees or the Angels – whatever team caught your fancy – and the guys working the souvenir stands were hawking these incredibly cute, hand-painted, funny-looking paper mache dolls of baseball players with heads that sat on top of metal springs and, well, bobbed around. That's what we're talking about – the aptly named Bobbleheads.

A buck, that's all they cost at the time. Practically giveaways. You bought 'em, you broke 'em, and you tossed them away. Only some people treated them like valuables. And guess what? They became valuable.

I'm talking about people like John Brey. John's a gregarious, good looking guy who plunged right into the insurance business after college thirty years ago. He even owned his own agency at one point up in Jersey. Made good money. Hated his job. Maybe that's why he was attracted to Bobbleheads. He says he'd look at them, and he'd just have to smile. Go ahead, take a moment and look at the pictures. Come on, you've got to be smiling, too. They're goofy, aren't they? But they're also innocent, and they reminded John of his childhood. Better times when his father would take him to see the Bronx Bombers. Mickey Mantle, Roger Maris, Yogi Berra. I could name the entire Yankee starting line-up, and I'll bet a lot of you can, too. John surely could.

John also remembers the first Bobblehead he ever bought. Who wouldn't, given the circumstances. He'd found a Los Angeles Dodgers Bobblehead doll that he just had to have. So he ordered it. The Bobblehead showed up from the dealer carefully packaged, but the little Dodger's head was cracked wide open. Looked like he'd taken a bean ball from the likes of Nolan Ryan. John remembers staring at the busted up Bobblehead and thinking "Maybe this isn't such a great hobby."

But he was dealing with a reputable dealer, so when he called him up to tell him that the Bobblehead was broken, John got his money back. That improbable beginning was John's first step to becoming King of the Bobbleheads.

But Bobbleheads weren't his first foray into the world of collectibles. He'd actually started, as an adult, by collecting baseball cards.

"I'd put sets together, then put them in plastic sheets, and put them in a drawer."

Can you hear John yawning? I think I can. But lots of people, including me, find card collecting exciting. John was just collecting to the beat of a different drum. In fact, he fancied Bobbleheads so much that he went to his tall, beautiful blonde wife, Diana, and said that he wanted to get out of the insurance business and start dealing them.

"Oh, no you won't," Diana said. "Not until you've paid for Matt's last semester of college."

Matt, as you might have gathered, was their son.

So John bided his time and collected Bobbleheads, and built an inventory like any good businessman. He built a website as well: www.nodderexchange.com (nodder is a nickname for Bobbleheads). And what was the first thing John did after writing that last check for college? That's right, he left the insurance business.

"I was out of there so fast," he said.

John accumulated more than just dolls as he waited for his son to start that last semester. He'd built up a real store of knowledge about the collectible of his choice. Back when he first started, most collectors were trading on eBay, so that's where John went trolling for Bobblehead treasure. Like most fans of the dolls, he was interested primary in the ones manufactured in Japan from 1960 to 1974. After that, he says the quality fell off dramatically. But for that fifteen year period, Bobbleheads were made from paper mache that felt like ceramic. They were also hand-painted in Japanese assembly plants.

"Some of the people painting them were real artists. They took a lot of pride in their work."

Most of the Bobbleheads were made for sports teams, and did not depict individual players, though there were notable exceptions: Willie Mays, Mickey Mantle, Roger Maris, and Roberto Clemente all had Bobbleheads made with their likenesses. So did some major historical figures, like Nikita

Khrushchev and Fidel Castro. In fact, those two Cold War buddies were marketed as "Kissing Cousins." Khrushchev had a tiny magnet in his cheek, and Castro had some metal in his lips. Get them bobbing close to each other and you can imagine the result, though maybe you'd rather not.

Another pair of smooching Bobbleheads – far more appealing than the kissing communists – was John and Jackie Kennedy. When they bobbed, Jack got the presidential peck. (Jackie always was an assertive woman.)

Chairman Mao Tse-Tung had a Bobblehead fashioned after him, too, though it's doubtful that the fanatics behind the Cultural Revolution would ever have approved of the Chairman's constant nodding to the running dogs of the worldwide Bobblehead conspiracy.

There were also a Cleopatra Bobblehead; a Charlie Brown *Peanuts* set, including Lucy; and tons of what John calls "ad dolls." There was a Bob's Big Boy Bobblehead (try saying that three times in a row), and a Bobblehead for a home builder called "Happy House." The state of Florida even had kissing oranges and kissing alligators as promotional Bobbleheads. And I almost forgot to mention that Colonel Sanders had a Bobblehead (Original Recipe, I believe.)

There was...ahem, even...an Adolf Hitler Bobblehead, which still strains John's credulity.

"You just know someone at the company saw that coming off the assembly line and said 'What are we doing? We can't be making this.'"

Even though few of the Hitler Bobbleheads were ever made, it never became a highly valued collector's item. John sold one of the few available for only $1000, but he says he was glad to see it go. "It was kind of creepy."

So John's seen quite a variety of Bobbleheads, but like most collectors, he's focused on the sports figures.

By the time he cashed out of the insurance business and headed south to the warmer climes of Florida, John had accumulated about three hundred Bobbleheads, and a vast trove of information about the dolls.

He owns a three bedroom house, and one of those rooms is devoted to his Bobbleheads. I say "his" but John would be the first to tell you that once you become a dealer, you're no longer a collector. He keeps a handful, as in four or five dolls, for himself, but that's it. Eight times a year he auctions off the rest; his stock is greatly augmented by collectors who consign their Bobbleheads to him.

About 98% of John's auctions take place online, and it's a rewarding business. He sells about a thousand Bobbleheads a year, and grosses about a quarter of a million dollars in sales. He's noticed some fascinating things about Bobblehead collectors.

"Most of them are about my age (John is fifty-two), and the Bobbleheads bring out the kid in them again."

And most of them, John says, don't have a problem with money. "They're doctors, dentists, lawyers, business owners. It sort of a higher end thing."

They may be professionals, or well financed business people, but John says his customers are "salt of the earth people. Very honest. I've never had a single bounced check, or someone bid and then not pay me."

Bobbleheads start at about one-hundred dollars, but the average price falls between three to four-hundred. John says the Bobbleheads, for some reason, attract addictive personalities.

"I can always tell when I've got a new collector because they'll be spending thousands of dollars bidding on ten different dolls."

John is there not just to sell them Bobbleheads, but to offer his expertise, which includes being able to spot the differences between a restored Bobblehead and one that's never been touched by a paintbrush or putty knife since it left the factory. "I can look at a picture of a doll and tell if it's an original in great shape."

He's quick to point out that there's nothing wrong with a restored doll, but they're worth notably less than an original doll in comparable condition.

How can *you* tell the difference? Go to John's website. He has almost a dozen different sections, including "Bobbing Head Repair Guide." You'll see lots of before and after shots of broken Bobbleheads, and stories of scams that unscrupulous dealers have pawned off on unwary buyers.

"The more my collectors know, the better I look and the better I do."

Some of John's customers have done extremely well. But the couple who got the biggest paycheck ever for a Bobblehead weren't even collectors. Jessica and Todd Moore bought an old, fixer-upper home in Seattle, a "war box house." That's what they call them up there. It's a square, two bedroom, one bath home originally built to house the workers at Boeing Aircraft during World War II. Jessica and Todd knew they'd have to put a lot of sweat equity into the house. The years hadn't been kind to it. Once it had been a deep, rich blue, but over the decades it had become as faded and sun-bleached as an old pair of jeans.

When they took ownership of the house, they were dismayed – as most of us would have been – to find that the owner hadn't bothered to clear out most of his "junk."

They spent days making trips to the dump, and hauling boxes of the old fellow's belongings to Goodwill. They finally worked their way to the garage, where they found a Washington Redskin Bobblehead.

"It was just sitting on a shelf with a bunch of old paint cans and tools," Jessica said.

She said that she'd seen Bobbleheads, but didn't take particular notice of this one. "I kept it, though, because I thought it was cute."

That amazingly valuable Bobblehead stayed right on that shelf in the garage for two years. "I never gave it much thought," Jessica said. "But then I started to wonder what it was. I brought it inside and looked online. I didn't see anything like it, so I stuck it in a closet."

Not just in the closet but *on the floor,* within reach of her two-year-old son, Corbin, who was crawling around every day. Cue the shark music from *Jaws* – DUM DUM DUM DUM...

The door opened and closed probably a hundred times in the next five months while the Bobblehead was in the closet. It's hard not to imagine the Bobblehead breathing a sigh of relief every time the door closed without the little Corbin taking hold of it.

"Then I went on line and looked again," Jessica said, "and I saw the little ones on eBay, but not the bigger one like we had." Much bigger. It was eighteen inches tall, one of the few promotional Bobbleheads made for store displays. "I didn't get very far figuring out what it was," admitted Jessica.

So she put it on Craigslist. "I figured maybe someone would tell me, saying something like 'I remember that when I was a kid.' I didn't put it up for sale, but I had seven replies in an hour, and one person asked if I wanted to sell it. Another guy gave me John's email address and website. As soon as I went to the site I saw what it was. Then I got excited."

Real excited: "I said to Todd, 'What if it's worth a $1,000?' And he said 'Hold on, *maybe* it's worth a hundred."

Jessica, undaunted, sent John a picture of the big Bobblehead, and then called him.

"John looked at the picture while he was on the phone with me and goes, 'Oh, yeah.' The conversation definitely changed."

They talked about auctioning it off, but then John told her that he had a client who would pay $8,000 for the Bobblehead.

"Who says no to $8,000?" Jessica remembered thinking. The old, "A bird in the hand is worth more than two in the bush," business.

But Jessica and Todd did say no. They went with the auction, and sold it through John for almost $18,000.

Jessica thinks that maybe, just maybe she became a little bit attached to the Bobblehead. See what you think. She named him Campbell. Why? Because she thought he looked so sweet, like the Campbell Soup kid. Before they shipped him off, she stood him on the dining room table and took a picture of him.

"I kind of miss him. But it's a great story."

Indeed, it is. The very first time Jessica and Todd came up with a collectible, they set a record for the highest price ever paid for one of those dolls. Kind of like the minor leaguer who gets up to the plate for the first time in the big leagues and hits a home run. It hardly ever happens, but it happened to them.

For John Brey, every day in the Bobblehead business is a great day. Back when he was an insurance agent, he remembers cringing when the phone rang. Now he picks it up and talks to people who share his passion. They know they'll find a willing ear, which is often harder to find than a valuable Bobblehead.

"Most of their friends and neighbors just don't get Bobbleheads. They look at a guy's collection and say 'Oh, that's neat.' But they're thinking, 'This guy's crazy. Get me out of here."

John understands them. And why wouldn't he? He's the King of the Bobbleheads.

Let's review our chapter, shall we?

1) Bobbleheads embody just about everything that's great with collectibles.
2) The dolls have appreciated a lot.
3) They're a quality product.
4) Collectors find that Bobbleheads give them a strong link to childhood.

5) New collectors of anything can lose control and buy too much.
6) Don't confuse a restored collectible for one in original condition.
7) You *can* find treasure in a garage or attic (just ask Jessica Moore).

And one more thing worth remembering from this chapter: John Brey is not only a true expert, he's enjoying the journey. So should you!

Now it's on to three household names that are among the very favorites of collectors: Mickey Mouse, Coca-Cola, and Superman. I'll even clue you into the strange, shady, secret life of the artist who drew the Man of Steel, and how the likenesses of Clark Kent, Jimmy Olson, Lex Luther and Lois Lane ended up in some very compromising situations.

Chapter 11
Comic Books, Mickey Mouse, and Coca-Cola

It's great to know that nice guys *don't* finish last. The nicest superhero of them all is none other than the one and only, the absolute original...*Superman*. The Man of Steel rules the world of superhero collectibles.

Hard to believe now, but the powerful superhero almost died on the vine. His teenage creators, Jerry Siegel and Joe Shuster, met on their high school student newspaper. The two young men tried for years to have their Superman creation published. Their final version of Superman came to life on a single night in 1934 when Siegel, the writer, and Shuster the artist, wrote and drew several weeks' worth of the superhero comic strips in less than twenty-four hours.

And then they started their own collection...of rejection letters from comic book publishers. Lots and lots of rejection. It's the proverbial story of artists and writers everywhere, and Siegel and Shuster had to bear witness to it for four long years. But what do we always hear about persistence? Something about it paying off?

In 1938, D.C. Comics editor Vin Sullivan was pouring through a pile of rejected comic strips that had been sent to him when Superman caught his eye. The rest, as they say – and never has that term been more appropriate – is history.

For collectors interested in investments, Superman is as solid as his pecs. The first appearance of Superman in Action Comics #1 in June, 1938 is now worth about $550,000 in near mint condition. The original price? (I knew you were going to ask.) Ten cents. But get this: even though the cover on the original Superman comic featured the Man of Steel, only the last thirteen pages of the comic book are actually devoted to his story.

But Superman made such a colossal impression on the reading public that he soon spawned the gold standard of superhero comic book series – and an entire array of collectibles: patches, buttons, puzzles, clothing, board games, utensils, toys of all types, lunch boxes, action figures, costumes, stickers, rings, belts, pillows and comforters, watches, necklaces... Trust me, folks, the super dude's debut eventually led to an amazing number of items. But it all started with that first comic, which eventually morphed into Superman of radio and television, the big screen, and video games (since 1978).

The first Superman comic whipped up more than a multimedia maestro and bazillions of collectibles. It also sparked the growth of a superhero industry that would eventually include many other collectible crime fighters: Batman, Spider Man, Captain America, Wolverine, Iron Man, Wonder Woman, Green Lantern, Human Torch, Mr. Fantastic, Hulk, Green Arrow, Professor X, Aquaman, Hawk Man, Super Girl, Luke Cage (without whom there would be no Nicholas Cage, remember?), Cat Woman, and many others. And all those comics are collectible.

Now the value of comic books depends on three major factors:

1) Rarity.
2) Condition.
3) Popularity of the character.

Alas, the popularity of superheroes began to lapse in the mid 1950s, so comic book companies pursued new themes – crime, war, westerns, and that perennial crowd pleaser, at least as far as some women are concerned, romance. You may also recall that it was about this time that "America's typical Teenager," Archie, first appeared, along with friends/love interests Betty and Veronica. Like Superman, Archie & Co. are still going strong today. And those early editions are still very collectible.

While Archie began to reign innocently and brightly over supermarket checkout stands everywhere, the artist who created Superman, John Shuster, sank into a darker realm. Almost broke, bitter over a vicious and unsuccessful battle for the intellectual property rights to Superman, Shuster began drawing different characters. *Very* different. Or were they? Hmmm, a more interesting question than you may think. But before I answer that question, let me tell you exactly what Shuster did when his career turned bleak. He drew *Nights of Horror*, a series of sixteen booklets that depicted lurid and illegal acts of sadomasochism. Now most people would consider Shuster's drawings mild by contemporary standards, but in the 1950s, Shuster's artwork led to the successful prosecution of the publisher under obscenity statutes..

But what's most interesting about the art of Superman's co-creator during this period didn't take place in a courtroom. In fact, it took place long before the obscenity charges were even filed. It happened right on Shuster's drawing board, because the men and women he created for *Nights of Horror* bore eerie – and widely noted – resemblances to...Clark Kent...Lois Lane...Jimmy Olsen...and Lex Luther, all of whom he placed in those compromising positions I mentioned a few pages back. It's enough to make you wonder if Shuster was trying to turn Superman into Super*stud?* Or was he consciously or subconsciously trying to get back at his publishers, to whom he'd lost that property rights battle? No one knows for sure, but what we do know is that the naughty men and women in *Nights of Horror* could have been stand-ins for the stars of the Superman series. In fact, Shuster's descent into the demimonde is the subject of a fascinating book, *Secret Identity: The Fetish Art of Superman's Co-creator Joe Shuster.*

Need I say that those sixteen booklets that Joe Shuster drew in his darkest days are now collectibles in their own right? Valuable because they are rare; the head writer even dumped the original manuscripts into the Long Island Sound to try to dodge vice detectives. Rarity, the first factor I listed in what determines the value of comics – and so much else – is also why Superman's premiere garnered more than a half million dollars in its last sale. But for collectors, the value of more recently published comic books has been a wild ride. Put on your cape and I'll give you a bird's – or maybe I should say a *Superman's* – eye view.

Most experts agree that starting in the 1970s, comic book publishers have been marketing many of their titles to collectors. They've done this using a number of techniques. It started with printing comics on high quality paper, but by the mid-1980s, when speculation in comic books was rampant, it also included special, foil-embossed covers and holograms. A lot of publishers even sold special plastic bags to protect comic book covers.

Speculation became so furious that there were numerous columns tracking the values of comics. There was a lot to follow. Print runs of hundreds of thousands were routine, and there were even print runs of several comics of more than *ten* million. And a lot of these comics were marketed to collectors.

It worked...for a while. But mostly it was a bubble, not unlike the housing or tech bubbles. And what happens to bubbles? That's right, they pop. The reason this happened to comics – and it happened big – is as basic as supply and demand. The former overwhelmed the latter, and the bottom dropped out of the market. We saw that with other so-called collectibles earlier in the book, and it happened again in the 1990s with those "special issue" comics.

Superman, however, and other superheroes from the 1940s to the 1960s – the Golden Age of Comic Books – were, in actuality, very rare. Why? Well, just like a lot of baseball card collections, millions of comics were thrown out. Countless millions more were recycled in paper drives during World War II. The net result was scarcity, the opposite of what happened in the 1990s when comics were printed with abandon. The inevitable drop in the value of latter day comics was so steep that two-thirds of all stores specializing in comic books closed. Not surprisingly, the print runs of comic books fell by as much as 90%.

Still, comic book collecting remains strong, and in my opinion it will always attract interest. Just look at the continuing popularity of comic book conventions, like the granddaddy of them all, San Diego's Comic-Con. It attracts 80,000 plus fans every year for a four-day celebration of comics, and it's only one of many comic book conventions held around the world. They're great places to discover a vast assortment of comics, and to talk with real experts.

Thankfully, there are newly-established companies that grade comics. Certified Guaranty Company (http://www.cgccomics.com/) and Professional Grading experts (http://www.pgxcomics.com/) have brought needed expertise to the rating of comics. That's made collectors feel more confident in their purchases.

If you collect comics, you'll have some stellar company, including Samuel L. Jackson, who gave Marvel Comics permission to use his likeness in the company's new Nick Fury series, and Ben Affleck, who played the comic book character Daredevil in the 2003 film of the same name.

Here are some tips on making sure the comics that you collect maintain their condition:

1) Store them in cool, dark places. Sunlight bleaches comic book paper. Heat and moisture can damage comics as well.

2) Avoid storing your comics in cardboard boxes, or using any materials to store them that contain acid.

3) Use the ever popular plastic storage bags. Many comic books stores sell them in bags. But even plastic isn't absolutely safe, so...

4) Use corrugated plastic boxes to protect best against acid, moisture, and vermin.

5) Yet another option is acid-free backing board and Mylar sleeves.

6) When framing comics, use glass that provides protection against ultraviolet rays, and archival quality frames.

You can bet the original Superman comic is well-protected. Any comic that you treasure should be protected as well, because it's important to you, not because of its investment potential, which, as you've seen, can be sketchy when you collect beyond the Golden Age of Comics. The takeaway message here is that comics are a blast, but don't get snookered by publishers – or manufacturers of other "collectibles" – who ballyhoo their products as investments...while they flood the market.

In that sense, the Golden Age of Comics remains...the gold standard. Why, even a 1954 Man of Steel lunch box recently sold for $12,000. (I'd call that a *gold* plate special.)

Mickey Mouse has carried more than a few lunches himself. He adorned the very first "character" lunch box in 1935, the dream child of Walt Disney himself. It's whimsical to look at, and expensive to own; the most recent sales had the rare Mickey "lunch kit," as they were called then, at about $2,000. Still a bargain compared to having Superman toting the P&B.

Mickey, like Superman, has given rise to an entire universe of collectibles, and it started very soon after the mouse's creation in 1928 by the twenty-six year-old Walt. The name, which rolls off our tongues so easily, faced an initial stumbling block. Walt was going to call the world's most famous mouse *Mortimer* Mouse. Fortunately, his wife, Lilly, had her way.

From Mickey's first appearance in the short cartoon *Steamboat Willie* to his latest incarnations on the big and little screens, and in every other media imaginable, Mickey has generated collectibles. When he was run for president, as a way to tweak the collective nose of traditional politicians, his buttons and bumper stickers were squirreled away. In 1957 the twenty-fifth million Mickey Mouse watch sold, but during the years 1967-1970, sales of the watches actually tripled because of the booming sales to teenagers and hippies – sometime, but not always, one and the same – poking fun at the establishment. Their value now ranges widely from $10 to $600 for the original Ingersoll-Waterbury watch. The big differences in price suggest the wide range of Mickey Mouse watches that were made.

The Mickey Mouse Club debuted in 1955 with those famous mouseketeer kids (Annette, Cubby, Bobby and the crew) and those equally famous mouse ears, which are yet another MM collectible. But what turbocharged the Mick's collectibles was the opening of Disney theme parks, first in 1955 in Anaheim, California, then in 1971 in Orlando, 1983 in Tokyo, and 1992 in Paris. As anyone who's ever taken a child to a Disney theme park can attest, there's no escaping without indulging the kiddies (or yourself) in some of the thousands of Disney items for sale, many of which feature Mickey and will become collectible in time.

Let's look at some of the earliest Mickey Mouse memorabilia. They include baby rattles, spinning tops, balls, pull and push toys, bedding, rocking chairs, bibs, panties, towels, and washcloths. Moving up the demographic ladder, we find children's items, such as toothbrushes, hair combs, pencil boxes, sharpeners, stamp pads, and rulers. And let's not forget more than a quarter of a million wind-up handcars, many of which featured Minnie as well as Mickey, that are reputed to have saved the Lionel Corporation from bankruptcy during the depths of the Depression in 1934. As with any collectible, the condition of these items is very important, as well as any original packaging.

Something to look for on the earliest Disney items was the way they were signed. From 1929-1933, Walt signed them Walt Disney, Walt E. Disney, Walter Disney, or just W.D. Then from 1934 to 1938, it changed to W.D. Ent., and Walt Disney Enterprises. In 1938 the signature changed once more to Walt Disney Productions.

The first important auction of Disney memorabilia was in 1972, when one-hundred-seventy lots were sold. Sales haven't slowed much since then. Here are the results of recent sales:

1) Mickey Mouse 1960s photograph: $76.
2) Coca-Cola tin tray celebrating Mickey's 75th anniversary: $10.
3) Mickey Mouse illustration from Disney Studios: $660.
4) Walt Disney signed drawing of Mickey: $561.
5) Mickey Mouse thimble set (yes, you read that right): $131.
6) Mickey Mouse toothbrush holder, 1930s: $96.
7) Mickey Mouse phone, 1970s: $120.
8) Mickey napkin ring: $132.
9) Mickey tin sand pail: $98.
10) Solid gold, two foot tall Disney stature: $4,000,000.

I'll bet that last item made you sit up and take notice. The statue – more than one-hundred pounds of solid gold

– was called *Celebration Mickey*, and was a key part of a huge effort to commemorate the birth of Walt Disney. The company sold the statue to raise money for charitable purposes, lest you consider the gold mouse the most outlandish act of corporate overindulgence on record.

Mickey Mouse has raised tons of money for charity. As former President Jimmy Carter once said, "Mickey Mouse is the symbol of goodwill, surpassing all languages and cultures. When one sees Mickey Mouse, they see happiness."

And I would humbly add that a lot of us also see collectibles.

I just mentioned the Coca-Cola tin tray celebrating Mickey's 75th anniversary (tin being a far more modest metal than the one used to note his creator's birth). It was no accident that Coke would have been part of such fanfare. Because Coke is such an American institution, that it too, has become an icon every bit as recognizable as its brethren in this chapter, Superman and Mickey Mouse, and just as collectible.

The logo for Coco-Cola, the uniquely curvy script, is instantly identifiable around the world, as is the contour shape of the bottle itself.

But in the beginning there was no...bottle. That's right. For Coke's first eight years, from 1886 to 1894, it was served only in pharmacies as a supposed cure for morphine addiction, dyspepsia, neurasthenia, headache, and even impotence (I'm leaving that one alone). The contour bottle was produced for the first time in 1915. You might think that owning one of those early, iconic bottles might be worth quite a bit, but you'd be wrong. That's because there were such vast numbers of the bottles produced, and they were sturdy enough to survive the decades. If you're old enough, you might recall that the glass was thick (hence, the perhaps dated reference to someone with "Coke bottle glasses.").

But lots of items from the early days are valuable. Toy trucks purchased for forty-nine cents in the 1930s are now worth thousands of dollars. A Victorian lady tray from 1897 is worth about $15,000 (trays, I should add, are among the most popular of all Coke memorabilia). A 1907 Coca-Cola calendar is valued even higher at $17,000. Even a calendar from 1922 is worth around $8,000. Let's look at a few more of the high-end Coke collectibles. A Coca-Cola clock and sign from the 1930s comes in at about $14,000, while a leaded glass shade from the 1920's will cost you more than $4,000.

A great guide to these prices is *Petretti's Coca-Cola Collectibles Price Guide.* In fact, if you're going to collect Coke memorabilia, I'd go so far as to say it's essential. The man knows his Coke. He figures a round thermometer from 1959 is worth almost $1,000, and he values a rare 1912 trolley sign at $12,000. He covers just about every Coke item imaginable.

But there are so many delightful collectibles at the other end of the price spectrum. One of my favorites comes from that immensely popular song from a Coca-Cola commercial in the 1970s. Is it playing in your head yet? Does this help: *I'd Like to Teach the World to Sing.* Yes, *that* one. Sheet music for the song, printed on a lovely graphic of the globe, would cost you only $10.

Here's a roundup of Coke collectibles with an emphasis on affordability.

Ad from 1955, framed and showing a pop machine: $10.
Bank, shaped like a 1950s Coke dispenser: $22.
Cap, red, for a soda jerk: $4.
Coke Santa doll: $100.
Flashlight, shaped like a coke bottle: $10.
Glasses, set of eight: $10.
Hinged box with bottles: $12.
Jug of Coke syrup: $15.
Tiffany style lamp: $45.
Coke bottle-shaped mold for Jell-O: $6.

Napkin dispenser, diner style: $30.
Ornament for Ozark Coke Club: $17.
Picture frame in the shape of the Coke bottle: $17.
Radio shaped like a Coke vending machine: $80.
Sign, neon in Coca-Cola script: $225.
Thimble: $4.
Water Globe, shaped like Coke bottle: $15.
Christmas cards, sixteen count: $10.
Yo-yo that lights up: $10.

Now, did you happen to notice that we darn near went from A to Z with that last list?

But it's easy to find like-minded, or perhaps I should say "Coke-minded" people. There's a huge community of collectors of memorabilia from this great American institution. And they're just as passionate as the folks who freaked when Coke tried to change the classic formula in 1985.

One of the most amusing stories I've run across concerned a fellow who took a woman on their first date to a convention of Coke collectors. They arrived a couple hours early, so he drove her around, eventually stopping outside a Coke facility. He wandered off, and when she looked up, all she could see was his bum just before it disappeared into a dumpster.

Now that's a true collector. At that point, she wasn't so sure about him or the activity that he'd chosen for their first date, but they eventually married, and they've been together ever since. And they're still attending Coke conventions just about every year, from what I've heard.

Not all of us will go dumpster diving for collectibles, but most of us have gone to lengths that might appear absurd to the uninitiated. But it's the thrill of the hunt. I can't say that often enough. Finding that one special treasure gets in your blood long before the collectible ends up in your hands.

Time to do a quick review.

1) Superman was the first superhero.
2) He gave rise to many other superhero crime fighters
3) He also gave rise to a huge collectibles industry.
4) He moved from comics to become a multi-media maestro.
5) His comics – and those of other superheroes – are widely collected.
6) The value of comics is based on rarity, condition and popularity.
7) Comics must be stored with great care.
8) Mickey Mouse appeared in 1928 for the first time in *Steamboat Willie*.
9) The world's most famous mouse quickly gave rise to a huge collectibles industry.
10) Disney theme parks turbo-charged the collecting of Mickey's memorabilia.
11) Mickey's most valuable collectible by far is a solid gold statue of him.
12) Coca-Cola remains a huge favorite of collectors.
13) Modestly priced Coke memorabilia covers a vast range, almost from A to Z.
14) Trays are among the most popular – and valuable – of Coke collectibles.

Collecting is, indeed, a journey, one that I've thoroughly relished. And now I'm going to give you a primer on one of my personal favorites: political memorabilia.

So all aboard for a whistle-stop tour.

Chapter 12
Buttons, Banners, and Lady Liberty

In the not so long ago, we heard from politicians with presidential ambitions only every few years. But nowadays, the modern media version of the whistle stop tour hardly ever stops tooting its horn between elections. It might get wearying for voters, but it's an absolute bonanzle for collectors of campaign buttons, bumper stickers, yard signs, and the scores of other items that are used to draw the attention of the electorate.

The history of American political memorabilia is as old as the country, and the items themselves provide snapshots of American life at each stop along the way. When George Washington ran for president, his partisans sported political buttons. But these were the *real* things. The buttons boosting his candidacy were made of brass and were sewn into clothes. In other words, they actually buttoned up the bearer. The ones snugging up George's backers said "G.W. – Long live the President." Sound familiar? It should because it was the new nation's take on "Long live the King." Switching political sides in those days must have meant hiring a seamstress, or breaking out your needle and thread (ouch!.)

In the eighteenth and nineteenth centuries, the types of political memorabilia put into play were generally limited to buttons and silk ribbons. It follows then, doesn't it, that collecting buttons is one of the oldest and most enduring obsessions of political junkies?

There have been three technological developments of note to the campaign button. The first was marked by the buttons worn by the supporters of the Father of Our Country, George Washington, as we've already noted. The second is marked by another giant of American history: Abraham Lincoln. That's because historians say the second phase of button development debuted in the 1860 campaign, which saw Abraham Lincoln pitted against Stephen A. Douglas.

Their race to the White House came two years after the remarkable "Lincoln vs. Douglas Debates" in Illinois, tough arguments that anticipated what we would call the "hot button" (as long as we're on that button theme) issue of the era: slavery. What's of great interest to collectors of political memorabilia is that tintype and ferrotype photo processes in the 1860 election made it possible for the first time to put the likeness of a candidate on a button.

An extremely rare campaign pin for Lincoln in 1864 shows the bearded president, and is worth about $650. Interestingly enough, buttons of the beardless Lincoln from his first presidential run in 1860 are even rarer, and therefore hold even higher values. Higher values for the beardless Lincoln even hold true for sheet music featuring "Honest Abe's" face on the cover.

But truth be known, even the buttons of this era weren't political buttons as we think of them now. They consisted of a metal ring around a picture. A hole was punched through the top, and then it hung from a supporter's lapel (generally) on a ribbon. From a historical standpoint, what's most noteworthy is that those buttons, along with other photos, made it possible for the first time for Americans living far from the seat of power to glimpse a likeness of a president or presidential candidate. To hold one is to hold history, and to see the first big step toward media domination of political campaigns.

Phase three of the button's evolution came in 1896 during the William McKinley, William Jennings Bryan campaign. That's when the political button, as we now know it, started showing up. Each candidate had his photographic image or slogan printed on a metal button with a pin in back. It would be reasonable to conclude that the advent of the first modern buttons in that *fin de siècle* race would make them immensely valuable, but I'm happy to say – for those of you who are just starting their collections (this is actually bad news for those of you who own McKinley, Bryan buttons) – that they were so popular and numerous that even now you can buy them for about $10, if you keep your eyes peeled.

Presently, we're witnessing a modest decline in the use of campaign buttons. Many political strategists have decided to put money into other areas. Be that as it may, buttons are both popular with collectors and fun. Just ask Ken Rodin, National Public Radio's political editor. He started collecting them at age fifteen. That would have been 1966, so he would undoubtedly have nabbed buttons for Lyndon Johnson and Richard Nixon. Fact is, I'd bet the house on it because Ken Rudin has now collected about 75,000 buttons. He even has an online column about his obsession: www.npr.org/blogs/politicaljunkie. Check it out. You'll learn a lot about collecting them.

Here's a tip from me about buttons: look for limited editions, as with anything else. When a political candidate barnstorms into a city or town, local organizers often print up their own buttons. Snap 'em up, and if you put them on, be careful. Condition, condition, condition is to collectors what location, location, location is to real estate agents. Please understand, I'm not saying to ignore the buttons issued by the national campaigns, especially if you like them, but those limited edition dandies are worth going after.

Another tip to keep in mind: short-lived national campaigns generally produce more valuable buttons. I'm thinking of the George McGovern, Thomas Eagleton ticket in 1968; Eagleton had to step down when it came out that he'd suffered serious emotional problems, which promptly drove up the price of their buttons, bumper stickers, and anything else with their names and mugs plastered on it.

One of the most valuable buttons of the last century is of President Franklin Delano Roosevelt when he was a *vice-presidential* candidate. Doesn't that sound counter-intuitive? In 1920, he played second fiddle to Democratic presidential candidate James Cox. They lost, and their buttons scattered like sparrows. Find the ones that perched safely over the decades, with both of their pictures on it, and you're looking at a cool $15,000 to $20,000, if it's in top condition (of course).

Which is not to say that political memorabilia was wholly limited in the first hundred thirty some years of our dear republic's life. Some historians feel that the great U.S. of A. actually invented campaign swag. Here's a mere sampling of the booty that was handed out to voters: toys; needles, thread, and thimbles; calendars; posters; pens; combs; paperweights; and hand mirrors.

Most assuredly, presidential candidates did not hand out locks of their hair, at least on a widespread basis, which surely explains, to a major degree, why the ones that are available are so rare and pricy. Case in point, President U.S. Grant: strands of his hair sold recently for $646. Staying high brow, a wooden campaign hairbrush from 1840 with the image of William Henry Harrison was auctioned for $4,431. (No word on whether there were any bonus hairs in the brush.)

Once political campaigns started roaring in the twentieth century, it was "Katy bar the door." The types of collectibles mushroomed so rapidly that the nonprofit organization American Political Items Collectors (APIC) formed in 1945. It has more than two thousand members, including Presidents Clinton and Carter, and, in APIC's own words, "is one of the oldest hobby organizations in the country next to coin and stamp collector organizations." They've even established a new Obama chapter, recognizing, I'm sure, the immensely historical nature of his election. APIC (www.apic.org) has regular newsletters, and is a superb source for information about political memorabilia and where you can find it.

While most of us would never go out of our way to promote smoking or drinking, politicians were less jittery about embracing those vices in the mid-twentieth century, and those attitudes led to some unusual political promotions. President Franklin Delano Roosevelt's campaign distributed shot glasses that read "Happy Days are Here Again" after the repeal of Prohibition, which had been part of his 1932 campaign platform. You can bet those shot glasses are worth more than the demon rum that once filled them.

In 1952, both candidates – General Dwight D. Eisenhower and Governor Adlai Stevenson – handed out promotional cigarettes (General Eisenhower, a four pack a day man at the time, had "I Like Ike," his popular campaign slogan, printed on the pack). Ike, as we all know, bested Adlai in the presidential race – and he's still beating him in the value of a pack of these old cigarettes by a comfortable margin of $139.95 to $109.95, according to the most recent prices – I almost said "polls" – available, the values of both "brands" would have been lower, if tobacco's notoriously addictive power hadn't done such an effective job of making sure most of those cigarettes were smoked within days of their distribution. The campaigns, I should add, also handed out far less toxic items, including pencils and potholders.

President Kennedy's campaign pushed a substance less habit-forming than tobacco when they printed up "Coffee with Kennedy" paper cups to encourage coffee klatches with the candidate and Mrs. Kennedy. What's the value of that cup now, *sans* java, about $100.

With JFK memorabilia, as with so much else with our thirty-fifth president, it's easy to move from the banal to the bizarre: a piece of upholstery from the Lincoln Continental that the young president was riding in at the time of his assassination went for $11,000.

The memorabilia in twentieth century American politics was rich and, yes, sometimes macabre. Often, it also reflected a president's more mundane predilections. Harry Truman's poker chips and playing cards were auctioned for more than $3,000, which would still be a pretty hefty pot at most Saturday night smokers.

You can generate your own memorabilia by bagging celebrity autographs during the ever-open campaign season – and I don't mean the politicians themselves. In the political biz, big name Hollywood Stars and Rock 'N Roll Royalty often go out and campaign for their favorite candidates. We've all seen that, right? They're called "stumpers," because they *stump* for their candidate. It's a perfect time to try to get an autograph from (most recently) Obama backers like Don Cheadle, Ron Howard, or Oprah Winfrey. On the Republican side, keep your eyes out for stars like James Caan, Pat Boone, or Ted Nugent. (Those last two have got to be the strangest bedfellows in rock 'n roll/political history.)

When you're stalking the stumpers, think ahead so you have them sign something interesting. In short, don't hand them a blank piece of paper. And forget your underpants because that's just plain tacky. But a baseball is always cool, and so is a program for a big fundraiser. And if at all possible, for authentification purposes get your picture taken with the celeb that does the signing.

Try to be diligent about your research as well. When John Kerry ran in 2004, a record album by *The Electras* was auctioned for $1,000. Why? It was Kerry's high school rock band. He played bass. But don't confuse the reissue that came out after his nomination with the original LP, because the reissue is definitely not worth a grand.

Another "don't:" don't forget those yard signs, either. Like buttons, they're usually cheap and plentiful, and are colorful additions to anyone's collection.

As with sports memorabilia or any of the other broad categories, you might want to think about narrowing your focus in the world of political memorabilia. You could collect only presidential losers, third and fourth party promotional materials, or historical documents of the various national political parties, such as drafts of campaign platforms. There are many areas in which to specialize and here again your own imagination could give rise to a category no one's ever thought of. The variety is extraordinary. Here's a list of just some of the items that come up for sale, and how you could develop them into a focus of your collection:

1) John F. Kennedy bookmarks: $6.99. Bookmarks noting historical issues and/or personalities are a wonderful specialty. So are the books themselves, so consider collecting first editions by major candidates, along with the bookmarks.

2) Peter Maxx signed 1993 Clinton Inaugural Poster: $650. I gave posters a brief mention earlier, but think about how you could structure such a collection (hints: by party, artists, or medium).

3) 1976 Republican National Convention Badge: $39. Political conventions are a great specialty because they're rife with collectibles, from badges to bunting, pennants to souvenir pens.

4) Historical newspapers: widely varied prices. The Los Angeles Times 11/26/63 edition has the unforgettable

headline: "Nation Buries Its Fallen President" and was available for $14. The U.S. has a lot of history and, in the past, it had a lot of newspapers. So there are lots of opportunities.

5) Historical magazines: again, widely varied prices. Look for the big names in magazines of old: *Life, Time, Look, Reader's Digest*; or specialize in smaller publications that have attracted readers for more than a century, such as *The Nation*.

6) Baseball cards with a man who became a political star. Now this is a sub-sub-specialty with perhaps only one member: Senator Jim Bunning, who starred for the Philadelphia Phillies. His cards generally go for less than $10.

7) Postcards of President Kennedy's assassination and postcards of other politically linked events. JFK's postcard, showing an aerial of Dallas, Texas, costs about $12.

But the postcard category that could really keep you busy belongs to none other than Lady Liberty herself. She rules the postcard kingdom. Those political parties come and go (just ask history buffs about the Federalist and Whig parties) but not the Statue of Liberty. She's stalwart and steadfast, and she's been the first beacon of the United States to millions of immigrants, extending hope for a new life in a land of freedom. And for collectors? Well, Lady Liberty represents a wealth of possibilities.

She's widely considered to be the best selling postcard of all time. Amazingly, more than three hundred forty publishers have produced more than fifteen hundred different postcards of America's most revered statue. There are photos taken from every conceivable angle, distance, and time of day or night.

Lady Liberty has also given rise to tons of statues that have been modeled after her. The most cherished (i.e. valuable) of all the statue collectibles are the ones manufactured in 1876 (the nation's centennial celebration), as well as from 1886, the year of Lady Liberty's formal dedication. Statues made in 1986 are also fine collectibles, celebrating, as they did, the good woman's one hundredth birthday.

One of the most desirable of all Statue of Liberty collectibles is a copy of the original 1886, four-page souvenir program for the dedication ceremony. Can't nab that one? Then go for magazines or newspapers of that time that described the ceremony. There's plenty of value in them, too.

Through the years a sampling of the types of Statue of Liberty items include pins, buttons, medals, candy containers, glassware, music boxes, models, banks, paperweights, cookie cutters, playing cards, sheet music, jars, bowls, men's ties, and books. Lady Liberty is so popular that there's a Statue of Liberty Collector's Club (http://statueofliberty-club.com/). Or you can call them at 1-800-266-1488.

Political campaign giveaways morph easily into historical memorabilia. The reason is obvious in a democracy: we elect our representatives and they proceed to make history. Let's take a few seconds here to review:

1) The 18th and 19th centuries saw limited campaign memorabilia, mostly ribbons   and buttons.
2) There were three phases in the development of campaign buttons: real   buttons, such as the ones worn by George Washington's backers; photos in small metal rings that hung from ribbons, such as the ones worn by Abraham Lincoln's supporters; and the modern day button with a pin in the back.
3) The most valuable buttons are ones from short-lived campaigns or the ones printed in small numbers by local campaign supporters on behalf of national candidates.
4) In the 20th century, the variety of political memorabilia has mushroomed (check out APIC).

5) You can create your own category of collectibles by specializing in a single area.
6) Lady Liberty reigns supreme among all political/historical collectibles.

Almost all collections can, and often are, passed down from one generation to the next, perhaps none so profitably – from an educational standpoint – than items of political and historical significance. In my next chapter, I'll look at the collectibles that appeal most to children, and I'll give you pointers on how to get them started. It truly is a joyful journey, so let's take the next step with the little ones in mind.

All aboard...

Chapter 13
Collectibles for Kids

"What's the matter with kids today..." Remember the song *Kids* from that huge Broadway hit musical *Bye Bye Birdie?* I suppose the answer to the question posed by the late great Paul Lynde is that nothing is the matter with kids today...but helping them get started with their own collection of treasured items might make *you*, the parent, actually ask that question a little less often.

The first and most important step you can take to help your child is to pause, *breathe*, and look at what your blessed offspring may have started collecting on his or her own. I've known parents who weren't even aware that their children had started collections, until I talked to them about it. (Heck, I've known adults who didn't even realize they were collectors until it was pointed out to them.) You might find that your child already collects insects, dolls, baseball cards, books, postcards, even rocks. My son started collecting baseball cards on his own at age five. Granted, I was certainly modeling the behavior of a collector for him, but he showed real passion for collecting cards at an early age (making me wonder if researchers will one day find a "collector gene".)

If your children have their collections simmering right along, all you have to do is help them turn up the heat by applying the tips and other information that you've picked up in this book. Your role will be to advise your kids, and avoid dictating much about what they're collecting.

If you've found that they're not collecting anything yet, the next step is to think about what they love to do. Does your daughter try to drag you off to every professional soccer game in the city? Maybe she'd like to save those ticket stubs or programs (maybe, unbeknownst to you, she already has) and start slipping them into a notebook that can hold her collection. Ticket stubs, as we learned in our chapter on rock 'n roll memorabilia, can become highly desirable collector items. This holds true for sports as well.

Do you have a boy who's wild about holiday ornaments, regardless of the time of year? Help him get going. There's no reason he can't collect and display them year round. The holidays are magical, and some kids like to keep the magic alive. For kids, anything can be a collectible: sewing sets, dolls, watches, books, music boxes, miniature dollhouses, playing cards, sports cards, butterflies (the renowned Russian-born novelist Vladimir Nabokov became a budding lepidopterist at age seven), books, diecast cars and trucks, patches from places they've been, stickers, flag lapels, marbles, video games, puzzles, handpainted soldiers, stuffed animals, cartoon characters, fastfood restaurant giveaway toys, ball caps, tee-shirts, travel mugs, key chains, souvenir pens and pencils... The great thing about kids' collectibles is the truly vast array of opportunities, and the way any collection can gather a family around a table.

Two especially popular items in the toy category are yo-yo's and spinning tops. It's estimated that about 500,000 different types of yo-yo's have been made; the earliest, wooden ones, are among the most valuable of all. As for those spinning tops, they're one of the oldest toys in the world. Tops have been made of wood, stone, metal, and plastic, and often depict colorfully painted soldiers, dolls, animals, and even circus and cartoon characters, such as Mickey Mouse, Yogi Bear, Bugs Bunny, and others. They became popular in the 1960s, and you'll find that spinning tops with cartoon characters are very collectible.

If your child hasn't started a collection, let me offer a couple of cardinal rules for helping them:

1) Make sure the collectible item you settle on isn't too hard to find. It has to be accessible, because the thrill of the hunt wears mighty thin with children if the hunt goes on too long. (Let me put it even more plainly: don't suggest collecting Dead Sea scrolls.)

2) Then make sure the item you're encouraging your child to collect isn't too expensive. Unless your pockets are really deep, most children aren't going to be super stoked about having a grand total of one or two items in their "collection." Kids, as I'm sure you've noticed, like quantity. *Lots* of stuff.

But, you might be saying, why should I want to encourage my child to collect "lots of stuff?" There's enough of it already bulging out of this old house of mine.

I'm going to take a moment here to address the "why" question, because it's an important one and deserves a thoughtful response. Children learn a great deal when they collect. They learn to be patient, because a collection most often grows piece by piece. They learn how to research the items they value, whether that means going on the Internet, or down to their local hobby shop or library. Sometimes it even means going to museums, both real and virtual. Or to a national park, if you're raising a young rock collector. Or to an ocean or river, if your son or daughter collects seashells; there are lots of opportunities with countless seashells scattered around the globe. All of these are great educational opportunities. And a child also learns about investing. Rare is the boy or girl who isn't aware that the money and/or time they spend on collectibles could yield greater value to their "holdings" with the passage of time. If that isn't a key lesson in finance – and life – I don't know what is. Then there's taking care of a collection – the careful ordering of the items and the means that children must undertake to protect their collectibles..

These are all important reasons to encourage your child to collect, but I have one more thought on what it does for a child, and I think this is the most important point of all: it helps children identify and develop a passion. It's so critical for children to find enthusiasms and cultivate them until they're just bursting with feeling. It can become the benchmark by which your child will measure his or her other passions in life. And if they don't learn to identify passion in childhood, it can become a lot tougher to do so when they grow up.

Maybe you've noticed that I haven't mentioned stamp or coin collecting yet. I've been saving them because they're two of the most popular subjects of kid's collections, and have been for many, many decades. And of course they still make headlines in the adult world, too, like this one that appeared recently in *The New York Times*: "$7.85 Million for U.S. Coin, and Extra for Stamp." The coin in question was a 1794 silver dollar that experts believe may have been the first United States dollar ever minted. The price established a new record. The Swedish stamp, which sold for an undisclosed price, was printed in 1857 in yellow instead of green; in the 1990s it became the world's most valuable stamp in a series of sales that reached almost $2.5 million at that time.

Stamps and coins are perfect vehicles for ushering your child into a world rich with history and art. And it's easy to access information on the Web, or in books and magazines, because stamps and coins have venerable collecting traditions.

The American Philatelic Society (APS), which began in 1886, has a section of its website (www.stamps.org/KIDS/ kid StampFun.htm) devoted just to children. It provides a lot of assistance but I have to be honest and tell you that APS' website will prove a tad stodgy for many children. I'd suggest to you take them to *Junior Philatelists on the Internet* (www.junior-philatelists.com) for a livelier presentation of the art and science of stamp collecting. It's geared wholly toward children. There's a substantial list of links right on the homepage to videos about stamps that celebrate trains, presidents of the U.S., and major holidays, along with many, many tips on how a youngster can get started, with all the "how-to's" a parent could possibly want. It's one thing to try to describe how to use a stamp hinge, for instance, but it's quite another to have a video present it to a child step-by-step. This website is a grabber, and it will appeal to most children. It even has a list of items a child might be interested in collecting *other* than stamps.

For those more inclined to use a book about stamps written especially for children, there are dozens of choices in bookstores, libraries, and at online booksellers. And don't overlook books that were published ten, or even twenty years ago, because even older editions of books about stamp collecting will contain verities unchanging with the times.

What is changing is our use of what is now quaintly referred to as "snail mail", and which inevitably invites speculation about the end of stamps as they've been known for so many centuries. It's quite possible, some would say even likely, that within your child's lifetime stamps will become as obsolete as telegrams. The U.S. Postal Service has experienced decreasing revenues for years because of the increasing use of email and other services. What that means for young stamp collectors is the opportunity to be, perhaps, among the last generations to stock up on contemporary stamps because as we all know, as a collectible becomes rarer, it also becomes more valuable.

Coins, on the other hand, are likely to remain minted for the foreseeable future. I could be wrong, but from what I've seen, people like to have at least some tangible money in their pocket. Regardless, the collecting of coins will continue long after the last penny is minted. Like stamps, people have collected coins – along with the quieter forms of cash – for centuries.

Coins are amazing. They can introduce a child to vast historical eras, geography, finance, world trade, and so much more. There's a good primer on coins at The United States Mint website (www.usmint.gov), which also has an entire section for kids and teachers (the latter could be you). What I particularly like about the Mint's website are the profiles of the sculptor-engravers who produce the magnificent art for those coins we cherish.

Children can easily narrow their focus to collecting only pennies, nickels, dimes, quarters, or, if they're feeling affluent, silver dollars. They could look at collecting foreign coins, which I would encourage as well because it sweeps them across thousands of miles and years of history. They'll learn about mint "marks," and might want to collect coins from only one mint. Or coins from the year they were born. Children can really identify with coins, which no doubt explains their great popularity over many generations.

Coins, like stamps, often become a lifetime activity. It can surely serve to gather family members around the table. There's something so mesmerizing about getting a long sought after coin. I've seen children stare in unbridled wonder at their find. (I've seen adults react the same way. In fact, in the spirit of disclosure, I've found myself hypnotized by a newly acquired collectible that I've wanted for years.)

The *Dummies* series has *Coin Collecting for Dummies* (also *Stamp Collecting for Dummies*). I think both books are terrific for children and adults just getting started with stamp or coin collecting. For about $22, they're packed with great tips on how to get your child interested in these activities. With coins, for instance, the authors suggest showing your child your own coins, if you've collected any at all, and then showing them the same coins in books. It also suggests exposing your child to coin collector clubs, coin dealers, coin shows, and coin auctions. It urges you to take them to a mint – many have tours – and to museums.

Suffice it to say that there are many compelling reasons that stamps and coins have been collected for centuries, and why millions of children worldwide continue to find these collectibles so attractive. And why so many of them end up collecting all their lives, and hand down their treasures to their children and grandchildren.

But whatever collectible your children become passionate about will enrich their lives immeasurably – and expand their notions of the world in ways too countless to measure. Even if their collections someday gather dust and lie abandoned, the lessons learned in this rich realm will last a lifetime.

Let's do our review, shall we?

1) Observe your children's interests to try to determine what they might like to collect.
2) If your children are not already collecting, try to guide them toward collectibles that are not too hard to find, and not too expensive.
3) Collecting helps a child learn patience, research skills, investing, and taking care of cherished items. Perhaps most important, it could help them discover a passion.

4) Stamps and coins have been collected for centuries, by both adults and children.
5) Great websites and books abound for young stamp and coin collectors.
6) Stamps and coins can teach children a great deal about many subjects, including history, geography, art, and biography.

Both you and your children will want to know how to take care of your collections, so in our next chapter we'll explore the "care and feeding" of your collectibles. That way your journey can continue in style.

Chapter 14
The Care and Feeding of Collectibles

A collection is a means of preserving items that are important to you and very often important to others as well. So you want to handle each collectible with care. That means making sure the items put their best feet forward, so to speak. You want your treasures to sparkle, but only if they should sparkle, such as a collection of crystal. A collection of vintage metal boxes, on the other hand, should look aged. You would never want to bear down with metal cleaners, by way of example, if that would eliminate valuable hallmarks. (For those of you unfamiliar with that term, it means a mark, used mostly in England, to denote gold or silver articles that meet standards of purity.)

Neither would you want to toss your collection of treasured teddy bears into a washing machine. And whatever you do, don't take your valuable glassware or ceramics and put them in a dishwasher. (I wince at the thought.) Use barely warm water to hand wash glassware and ceramics. I'm big on keeping your items free of dust, and using only a damp cloth for cleaning.

Most of us take care of our collectibles so we can display them at their best. Now, not all people want to display their collections. Remember the fellow who collected thimbles who'd been made to feel self-conscious about what other people considered his odd obsession? He kept his thimbles– literally and figuratively – in the closet. Other collectors may not be eager to display or – as they might see it – *flaunt* their affluence. Or they might be worried about having their valuables stolen.

But most of us do like to share our passions; humans, after all, are social creatures first and foremost. And what better means of socializing than by introducing friends and acquaintances to the delights that you have collected? They are conversation pieces *par excellence*.

This raises the question that every new collector faces: How do I display my collection? I'll start by saying that when you begin to collect, it's easy to display every item you acquire. But you will find that as your collection grows, you'll need to become more selective about what you put on display. That's not such a challenge if you're collecting small items, but if the actual size of the collectible is a factor, this can become a huge (pun intended) challenge. Some folks solve this problem by rotating their items in and out of view every few months. Others show off only their finest pieces.

At the same time that a growing collection can force you to think twice about what to display, it can also tame your wildest impulses to buy items that, strictly speaking, are outside the purview of your interest area. You begin to consider how the piece that you just spotted will look alongside your existing collection. In some cases, you'll realize that you're asking yourself that old question from your school days – Which of the following items does not fit? – and reaching the painful conclusion that the answer is the item for which you're about to empty your wallet.

When this happens to you, you're being reminded of a key to great collecting: self-discipline. A bargain isn't a bargain if it's not something you need.

When great collections are displayed, they will show focus, theme, along with a hint of serendipity. I've been collecting for decades, and I've learned quite a bit about displaying my finds. I applied a lot of those lessons before I opened my museum in San Diego, which a journalist once described it as "part Cooperstown, a shot of the Rock 'n' Roll Hall of Fame with a big twist of the Smithsonian, to a Beatles soundtrack" (I'll have more about my museum in the afterward). I've also been privileged to view the private collections of scores of people. I've seen what works and what doesn't. Ready?

Instinctively, collectors tend to group their items together. For example, a sports collector may group all jerseys in one area, all baseball cards in another, feeling that if you spread them out in different locations in a room, viewers will lose the force of a particular collectible. There's validity to that way of thinking, but you can get creative with your displays without losing the power of iconic items. As I noted at another point, I like to form a group of varied collectibles around an individual athlete by placing his jersey, signed baseball, baseball card, and statue in a single arrangement. Now I'm not suggesting that this is equivalent to Picasso's extraordinary composition in *Three Women,* but it suggests that you needn't become rigid in your approach. In effect, what I've done is group by player as opposed to item. You could as easily group by team. By MVP awards. By century. You can create the rules for displaying your collectibles, just as you can create the rules about the items that you're collecting.

On the other hand, when you have a treasure of significant historical value, you might be wise to set it aside as a means of subtly suggesting to visitors that this really is worth slowing down for. I am fortunate to have obtained one of the very few authenticated T206 Honus Wagner baseball cards issued between 1909 and 1911. Having a special place for a card widely revered in card collecting circles has a practical value, too, and here's a quick anecdote to demonstrate that point.

When my museum was under construction, I showed the Wagner card to one of the builders. Had the museum been finished, I would have led him to the display case. Instead, I brought out the card to show it to him...and a few moments later misplaced it. You can imagine my throat-choking panic. One minute one of the most valuable base-ball cards *in the world* was right there in my hand, and the next minute it was *gone!* I found it a while later under a piece of paper, and felt a flood of relief. But you see, in my enthusiasm about the T206 Wagner, I violated one of my key rules for displaying an item: have a place for your valu-ables, and don't move them about casually.

Not only have a place for them, it's a smart idea to devote a single page to list the identifying features of the collectible, along with a clear photograph of it, and details about exactly where you've displayed it, right down to its position on a shelf or wall. This last suggestion may seem over-the-top to a new collector with relatively few items, but if you get in the habit now of documenting your col-lectibles in the manner I've just described, including the positions they occupy on shelves or walls, you won't have to go back and do all that work later. And when it comes time to insure your collection – yes, we'll get to that, too – you'll probably have to provide all those details to the bean counters. I'd also recommend keeping your records in a location removed from your collection. A bank safe deposit box will do the trick.

Shelves or walls? Ah, yes, we get to the actual place-ment of your collectibles. Items that are intended to be read, like historical documents, are best viewed on walls. This category would also include newspapers and magazines with famous headlines, and a sports jersey; who really wants to see Willie Mays' game-used jersey folded up like a Hathaway shirt in a department store? You want to see every bit of the Say Hey Kid's jersey, including the scuff marks. Need I add that you should frame documents, jerseys, and the like with special glass to protect them against light? (No push-pins *please*.)

Baseballs, dolls, music boxes, die cast cars; all stand out handsomely on a shelf, as do hundreds of other collectibles that are brazenly three-dimensional. I think once you have the principle here you're on your way. It's all about visibility, and as long as you keep that in mind, you'll be fine.

It takes time and some money to make your collection a real showcase, but as a newbie, don't let yourself become intimidated by all this talk about shelves and frames and documentation. A collection happens step-by-step, and so do your efforts to display and document your treasures. You might find yourself surprised by the glow you feel when you step back and look at your budding collection, after you've carefully displayed it. Believe me, it's a tangible sense of accomplishment, heightened when others come to visit and you see them admiring the care that you've put into your treasures.

You protect your collectible when you display them properly, but that's not enough. You also need to be concerned about creating a stable climate. No, I'm not talking about global warming, I'm talking about making sure that you keep your collection at a comfy sixty-eight to seventy-two degrees, with as little variation as possible. I try to keep my collection right at seventy. How important is this? Well, for every ten degree drop in temperature, the life of paper is doubled. If it's toasting at ninety-five degrees – not uncommon in summertime attics – you're destroying the value of that newspaper with a famous headline. This is why you never, ever want to put your collectibles in an attic or basement. Dust, grime, and food particles are the enemies of collectibles. If you must store them, keep them in a closet, and keep them comfortable; they like the same temperatures you do. And keep the humidity low and constant, preferably no greater than fifty percent. Mold and fungus just love high humidity, and when humidity rises those little buggers will climb right under your frame and go to work on the Say Hey Kid's jersey. Your collection is also subject to attack by bugs, such as termites. So you should be watchful. Not paranoid, mind you, but aware.

I've mentioned the need for glass that protects against sunlight, but the best protection is to never expose your collectibles to direct sunlight at all. For a few years, you probably won't notice any problems, but time, to paraphrase one of Mick Jagger's earliest lyrics, is not on your side: continued exposure to direct sunlight will make just about anything except human skin fade. It will even damage signatures on baseballs, especially if they've been signed with a regular ballpoint pen or, heaven forbid, a pencil. That's why I recommend a Sharpie, but Sharpies haven't been around that long. I have professional basketball programs from the 1960s with signatures in pen, and already there's considerable fading. Likewise, I have a presidential land grant bearing the fading signatures of President Thomas Jefferson and Secretary of State James Madison. That document is more than two hundred years old, and still reasonably legible, but again, the deterioration of the signatures is obvious.

You're faced with a real dilemma regarding signatures. It's natural to want to share autographed balls and the like with others, and to do that you have to display them. But when you display them, you do expose the signature to the slow ravages of light. My advice is to display your objects as safely as you can; and by the way, that means out of the hands of young children.

Now let's talk about insurance. I know it's not the most scintillating subject, so I promise to keep it short and to the point. But first let me put insurance needs into perspective.

If you're collecting refrigerator magnets, you get a pass on what follows because you do not need to insure them. The same could be said for most Bobblehead collections and die cast toys. Relax, enjoy your collection, and unless you know more about these items than I do, don't sweat the insurance premiums.

On the other hand, if you've collected limited-edition books, or stamps or coins, than you should probably give insurance some serious thought. Here again, common sense comes into play. Look at your collection and evaluate it soberly. Then ask the question we should all ask when considering insurance: is the cost worth it?

I've already stressed the value of devoting a page for each collectible that details what it is. You'll want to note size, condition, value, provenance, and whatever sales receipts you might possess for it. But please note that most collectibles rise in value, so a five-year-old sales receipt will not be the value that you'll want to insure it for. The receipt simply adds authenticity to your record of the collectible. Better to have a current appraisal and restoration expense, along with whatever other expenses you've incurred. Speaking of authenticity, remember those Letters of Authenticity, the LOAs that you received from wherever you bought an item? Include them, too.

These records, incidentally, will serve you well if you ever decide to sell a particular item, much less your entire collection. Potential new owners will want to know as much about a collectible as you would.

Some new collectors are under the impression that their homeowner's insurance policy will cover their collection. Frankly, I thought so as well. And some homeowner's policies do cover them, but most do not. They'll cover fine art, but even a serious art collector may still want to have a special fine arts insurance policy. But many other valuable collectibles won't be covered by a homeowner's policy. The surge in collecting is relatively new, so insurance companies may start to include them in standard homeowner policies, but don't bet on it in any sense of the word. Check, and then double-check. Then ask yourself if the amount of the coverage will actually protect against the real value of your loss. And be sure to see what types of hazards are covered by your policy. If your collection gets carried away by a flood, your policy might not cover it.

There are a number of insurance companies specializing in collectibles, including the Collectibles Insurance Agency of Westminster, Maryland.

Now here's a pleasant surprise: special collectibles insurance, whether it's for fine art, sports items, pop culture, presidential memorabilia, or any other high value items, will probably cost less and be more comprehensive than a standard homeowner's policy. Hooray for that! As a broad benchmark, figure about two dollars for every one-thousand dollars of coverage, which translates into about $2,000 a year for $1 million of coverage. The premium cost can be higher, up to ten dollars for every $1,000 in coverage, depending on your circumstances.

Make sure you know whether you'll be covered for items that you pick up while traveling. And when you shop around for coverage – always advisable – also make sure that you're dealing with an "admitted" insurance company. That's a firm which has been approved by a state's insurance department. If an admitted company gets in major financial trouble, a state may take over its operations and pay claims from a guaranty fund.

This may sound like a dry, academic subject, but let me assure you that the real life ramifications of insurance coverage can turn fierce as fire. I know. I had as close a call with the total loss of my collection as any collector will ever want to experience.

As I've said, my museum is in San Diego. One October a wildfire burned so close to my museum, that I was forced to evacuate and left having to make some fast decisions about what I'd take with me. Definitely, that Honus Wagner T206 baseball card. It's small, portable, and arguably a national treasure. But you don't want to find yourself trying to make decisions on irreplaceable objects when a wildfire is blazing at your back door. Fortunately, those true heroes of our community, the firefighters, fought off the flames; I was left with just a char mark on my property. Smell the smoke once, though, and the need for insurance takes on real meaning.

So have smoke alarms, but sadly, fire isn't the only threat: The FBI reports that a burglary occurs every fifteen seconds in the U.S. (that's more than 1.5 million home invasions a year). So once your collection starts gaining real value, it's smart to consider an alarm system, if you don't have one already.

There, I've covered those pesky issues of insurance and alarms, and we've considered your options for displaying your collection. Time for the review.

1) Err on the side of caution when cleaning your collection so you can display your items at their best.
2) As your collection grows, so do your display challenges.
3) You may group items around many themes. Collectors can be as creative with their displays as they are with what they collect.
4) Displays keep treasures in assigned places; therefore, these valuables are less likely to get misplaced.
5) Devote a page to the particulars of each collectible, and include a clear photo and pertinent documents, such as LOAs.
6) Walls are excellent for displaying items that must be read, such as documents; shelves work well for items that don't lie flat.
7) Temperature and humidity must be regulated to provide for a stable climate for your collectibles.

8) Never store your collectibles in an attic or basement.
9) Always use protective glass; regardless, avoid direct sunlight.
10) Consider your insurance needs, then shop around carefully.
11) Make sure you have security and smoke alarms.

Back to the fun by going back to the future. That's where we're headed on the next step of our informational journey. We'll look at the future of your collection by considering what part of the present and past you might consider collecting now.

Chapter 15
Collecting the Future Now

Will the collectibles industry continue to exist and thrive? I'm asked that question all the time, and for anyone starting out as a collector, it's a legitimate concern. You don't want to get yourself all fired-up for what might be a passing fad.

These issues are particularly pointed during sluggish economic times, so it's important to keep in mind that collecting is a unique passion driven largely by people who have the means necessary to purchase the items they desire. That said, let me add that economists believe that most Americans have cut back on their spending.

On the other hand, some of the prices that people are paying for collectibles are truly astounding. *Sports Illustrated Magazine*, for example, reported the following recent auction results:

-- A dentist paid $7,475 for Ty Cobb's dentures.
-- Two pieces of bubble gum chewed by former Arizona Diamondbacks outfielder Luis Gonzalez sold for $10,000. (You read that right, *chewed up* bubblegum!)

-- Soccer player David Beckham's shoes sold for $3,418.
-- A straw hat worn by Babe Ruth went for $6,065.
-- The Super Bowl ring of Chicago Bears' William "The Refrigerator" Perry sold for $27,473.
-- A piece of wedding cake from Joe DiMaggio's wedding to Dorothy Arnold, (not to Marilyn Monroe), in 1939 went for $1,742.
-- The 70th home run baseball hit by Mark McGwire in 1998 went for $3.1 million. Even some non-sports items have jumped into the act in a big way. Check out these recent prices:
-- A first edition book copy of "The Cat in the Hat" sold for $6,900.
-- A photograph of the "Dewey Defeats Truman" headline from the Chicago Tribune "forecasting" the 1948 Presidential election victory, signed by Harry Truman, sold for $9,200.
-- A "Ski at Mount Mansfield" poster by Stern Voorhees sold for $3,680.

You may be shaking your head, wondering who in their right mind would pay those kinds of prices. I mean, really, who would spend $10,000 on used bubblegum? Or $15,000 on basketball great, Michael Jordan's drivers license? The answer is a lot of people, or the bidding would never have risen that high. And it's likely that in our celebrity saturated culture, people will continue to spend serious money on the stars they idolize. But I also think, and so do a lot of other experts, that as Baby Boomers age and retire, they'll have more time to devote to their collections or start new ones.

Lest we forget, there are a growing number of items being auctioned at a growing number of websites, which strongly suggests that this is an industry around for the long run. Now I must admit, when I first started collecting as an adult, I worried that I might be plunging into a passing phenomenon. I think that's a widely shared concern among newbies, but I've been in the business long enough to have concluded that this is simply not the case. If anything, there are more collectors than ever out there.

So what does the future hold for the collectibles themselves?

I'm not a seer, and I definitely don't purport to foretell the future, but I can offer you some good bets on what to collect now.

First, political items almost always become collectibles. Yup, those buttons, stickers, tee-shirts and other essentials of campaigning that we talked about earlier in the book are worth nabbing for the future.

Second, video games and game systems will become collectibles. This is inevitable because there is always new technology replacing the old standard, and "gamers," as they're called, will need to constantly update their video library to stay on top of what is new and unique.

Holding on to outdated versions can be a valuable habit for collectors of other marvelous electronic gadgets as well. But to get the most bang for your buck, you'll want to hold on to more than just the device. To illustrate what I mean, let's talk about iPods.

It seems that every year or two many of us find ourselves pulling out our wallets to double our gigabytes or nab the newest features. The next time you upgrade, do yourself a favor by saving not just the old iPod, but all the packaging and labels and price tags – I mean *everything* – for the *new* one. The next time you upgrade your iPod, you'll be able to stick what will become your old one into its pristine plastic case. Then you just have to put it away until time works its wonder.

I can't overstate the extra value you'll receive by having collectibles in their original packaging, regardless of the item.

Posters are also a good bet for the future. I'm talking about a wide array of them – movies, sports, rock 'n roll, even travel destinations. There are new films released year in and year out, and it's well worth collecting original posters for movies that could become classics. Of course, you don't know it's a classic at the time, even when film reviewers call a film an "instant classic," a much overused term. But keep in mind that posters for films with actors who might become superstars will also rise in value. Check with your local theatre to see what they do with their posters after a film has had its run. And find out what your local video store does with those posters for films when they come out on DVD. At my local store, they're placed in a bin and given away for free.

The same holds true for rock 'n roll. How would you like to own a poster for The Beatles at The Cavern club in Hamburg, Germany? My advice, in short: catch a rising star. Become your own talent scout.

In sports, the Super Bowl is an excellent example of how every year produces new posters of the championship team. New gridiron stars often emerge, too.

Now, you might think that travel posters would be less susceptible to the tides of change, but they're always getting updated. An old poster of Aspen will soon be replaced by a new one shot from a different angle, or depicting an entirely different scene. Then guess what happens? The old poster reminds people of days gone by, and becomes a collectible.

Think about collecting tickets to major events, and always hold on to tickets for professional sports. Going in the gate, you have no idea whether a major record will be set or broken. But if it turns out to be a memorable day, you'll want that ticket stub...and so will others in the future.

Likewise, save those ticket stubs to concerts by major rock stars. And if for some reason you can't make the event, save the entire ticket.

You might be tempted to turn your nose up at the toys that are given away by fast food restaurants, but don't.

McDonald's has handed out tons of them (literally), and the value of these freebies has grown tremendously precisely because so many people didn't take them seriously and tossed them away.

Porcelain figures from companies such as Royal Dolton and Lladro, among others, almost always become collectibles. Both companies offer exquisite lines, including limited editions. Lladro produces many amazing creations, including fantastic dragons, horses, and a porcelain monkey with an unforgettable expression. In the case of Royal Doulton, certain Toby jugs, which feature intriguing faces from the olden days, are manufactured each year in finite numbers. But like the Lladro products, these jugs can also be a bit pricy, so you'll have to be willing to spend money now in the hope that down the road you'll make it back...and then some. Meantime, you're building a bigger, ever more beautiful collection, which is satisfaction enough for most collectors.

Another sure bet are Disney items. They've always been immensely popular, and there's no reason to think that they won't remain so in the future.

Music boxes, snow globes, even currency are all worth considering when you're thinking about the future of collectibles. And don't forget that old standby: trading cards. This is one of those no-brainers because sports memorabilia collectors will always snap up the next available set of cards and those new sets will always be hoarded.

Try to stay aware of the big news stories of our time. The O.J. Simpson trial became a haven for collectors. There were not only newspapers with their huge headlines about Simpson, but also buttons and stickers and books about the case. The Watergate affair produced a mini-industry within the realm of political memorabilia. So did Vietnam. It's wise to keep an eye on the signature events of our time.

We do live in an historic era. People always say that, but with the election of Barack Obama we've been reminded of this in the clearest terms possible. Look for the next Obama, but don't dismiss anyone rising on the national political stage. Think for a moment about the value of those locally produced Sarah Palin, John McCain buttons, if someday we're referring to a President Palin. (Please understand that I'm not advocating anything but wise collecting here. And do keep in mind that the most valuable political button of the twentieth century came out in 1920, when FDR was the vice presidential candidate on the Democratic ticket.)

When considering the future of collectibles, it's always a good idea to turn your anthropologist's eye on children, and ask yourself a very simple question: What do my kids and their friends like to play with?

Keeping that in mind, I want you to ask another question: Of the toys and games and so forth that they like the most, which of them embodies the era in which we live?

That's what you should consider collecting. And let's hope those items aren't the pricier ones on store shelves, because I'm going to suggest that whenever you can, buy two of each of those collectibles. Let your child have one to play with (and batter to pieces, if she or she is so inclined), and quietly put away the other one, leaving it to nest nicely in its original packaging with all the labels still tightly attached. That's right, put it in the back of your closet and toss a spare duvet over it. Or better yet, hide it up on a shelf where the youngsters will be even less likely to find it.

Please understand, I'm not suggesting that you buy duplicates of everything, or even most things. Do it only for the few items that really capture the times in which we live, like those lunch boxes did in the 1950s, the ones with Davy Crockett and super heroes on them. If your mom or dad had bought one and put it away, you'd be sitting on an extra $10,000 or more right about now, for what would have been a tiny initial investment.

But I'm not scolding the seniors because, as I said, the collecting surge was still years in the future.

And don't forget those McFarlane Sports Picks figures I noted a few chapters back. For a small investment there's a world of potential.

Above all, try to avoid getting caught up in a craze. Beanie Babies are a good example of this. I mentioned them earlier. If you weren't part of the frenzy, it's hard to believe how utterly extreme it became back in the 1980s. The manufacturer was very successful in its primary goal: selling Beanie Babies. But for most collectors of the toy, the strategy proved far less fruitful because it turned into yet another case of a company driving sales by marketing the collectability of its product. The result for collectors? So many Beanie Babies were sold that the market became saturated with them. You can hardly give away the creatures now.

It's hard to imagine collectibles centered on popular music losing their value, so in addition to saving those concert ticket stubs and posters, take a second look at your old LPs. Make sure you're not selling them short if and when you lug them out for a garage sale. Look at CDs with a fresh eye as well. They'll be outmoded in the foreseeable future, and there's no reason to think some of the most famous and influential recording artists of our time won't be worth collecting on CD, as they have been on vinyl.

How about women's fashions? The slit skirt really spoke of the eighties. What speaks for our era? Hard to say right now, but here's a tip I love to share: Every week in the online New York Times fashion section, photographer Bill Cunningham has a slide show called On the Street in which he posts photographs of street fashion in Manhattan. You may not live there, but there's no denying that New Yorkers set a lot of fashion trends. Cunningham focuses mostly on women, but he turns his lens on men on occasion. He makes logging on well worth it, even if you don't decide to save your fashionable clothes or accessories.

Speaking of men's fashions, sneakers have emerged as a hugely popular collectible. "Sneakerheads," as they're called, are mostly men, some of whom collect hundreds of pairs. The focus – no surprise here – is on basketball and tennis shoes. Much of the popularity of the sneakers followed the huge surge in the popularity of basketball and hip hop music in the late 1980s. How would you have liked to have snapped up a first generation Air Jordan, fresh out of the original box?

You didn't? Well, neither did I.

Do you remember in the beginning of this book when I suggested you look around your house to see what kind of collectibles you might already own? Now I'm going to suggest that you go directly to your pantry and take a close look at what you're eating and drinking. Do you have a handsome tin of tea that you're about to finish? Does it have "organic" written across the top in a lovely script? I suspect that organic food products that don't turn funky (tea in a tin won't) – and some organic clothing with the labels attached – will increase in value because they speak to the changing food habits and consumer choices of our era.

When you're considering the future of collectibles, it almost always pays to look at publishing. Madonna's book, *Sex*, published in 1992, is still highly sought after. What can we garner from this example? The combination of celebrity and sensationalism is a likely collectible winner. And always get a first edition hardcover. That's a maxim worth remembering.

Let's go for our final review.

1) Collecting is not a passing fad.
2) Prices for many collectibles remain astoundingly high.
3) Electronic devices such as video games and iPods are worth saving (and always keep the original packaging).

4) Hang on to posters for movies, sports, rock 'n roll, and travel.
5) Ditto for tickets to major sporting events and rock concerts.
6) Don't toss those fast food restaurant toys.
7) Disney items and porcelain figures have a long history of maintaining their value.
8) Keep an eye on the big news stories of our time, and rising political stars.
9) Look at the toys that children play with.
10) Try to avoid crazes, like the Beanie Babies.
11) Look at first edition books, especially by celebrities.

And now I'm going to give you the most important tip of all: collect what you love. It's what I said at the beginning of this book, and it's worth repeating now. If you love the items that you acquire and choose to display, others probably will, too. And even if they don't, this is your indulgence. Don't ever forget that.

And don't ever forget this: Enjoy the journey!

Afterward

Collecting has provided a long, joyous journey for me, and a great blessing. I've been collecting for more than half a century. Before I date myself too much, let me mention again that I started collecting cards when I was still a young boy. I can still remember carefully opening each new package of "bubble gum baseball cards" – that's what we called them – and smelling the pink wafer, which left a fine layer of dust on the top card. I'd look through each of them, reveling in the scent of the gum and hoping, *hoping* that one of the great players would be in the packet. Not some guy who was a .240 hitter, but a Mantle, Maris, or Mays. Or a Bob Gibson or Clete Boyer (now that I think of it, Boyer *was* a .240 lifetime hitter, but one of the great Golden Glove winners of all time.)

When I came upon one of those cards, or a Roberto Clemente, Rocky Colavito, or Robin Roberts, I felt like I'd found the Holy Grail. Did I treat those cards with undue reverence? I don't think so. I treated those cards like the treasures they were, and the treasures they would become, thanks to my mother. As I said earlier, she squirreled them away long after I'd forgotten them. And when I was ready – a man settled in his adult life – she gave me one of life's greatest gifts: she gave me back a marvelous part of my childhood.

Those cards that I'd carefully collected filled several shoe boxes, and most of the cards were almost as crisp as they were when I'd opened up each new package of bubble gum. I'll admit that I lifted up the boxes to see if even a faint trace of the gum remained. Only in my imagination.

But those cards were real, and they were valuable. My childhood collection pump-primed my adult passion. I started with those cards and moved over the years into many different kinds of sports memorabilia: game used jerseys and jackets, gloves, bats, balls, and hats. In time I would acquire one of those incredibly scarce Honus Wagner cards; Wilt Chamberlain's rookie uniform; autographed hockey gear from the incomparable Wayne Gretzky; and baseball items that once belonged to the near mythical man himself, Babe Ruth. When I found myself branching into rock 'n roll, I could hardly believe that I held – much less owned – the glasses that John Lennon wore on the cover of *Sgt. Pepper's Lonely Hearts Club Band.* And when I started looking at other pop culture collectibles, I was utterly delighted to get the late Christopher Reeve's cape from his first Superman film. I felt the same way when I obtained the original script of *Casablanca,* Humphrey Bogart's most notable film. You see, one passion led to another, and it wasn't long before my interest in historical collectibles was sparked, too.

I learned a great deal about my country by collecting bits and pieces of its history. It's impossible to obtain the signatures of every president, as I've been fortunate enough to do, and not become curious about the grand hopes and deep disappointments of our greatest and, in some cases, our most befuddled leaders. Likewise, I've lived anew many of the most fantastic games in sports by finding a memento of those superb moments. Collecting rock 'n roll memorabilia has also served to bring to life the great artists who have died; and, in a profound way, those collectibles have also made me appreciate even more the amazing achievements of the men and women who have

survived through decades of touring and recording and living the often tumultuous life of a rock 'n roll hero.

Collecting, you see, has made me realize that I'm part of
something much bigger than myself – the vast cultural and
historical currents that have flowed into our present era.

But it's also taught me lessons about setting personal limits, and talking to the people whom I'm closest to about
how far I can go with my collecting fever. I've been fortunate, because in my case my passion led to my building a
museum, the one described by a journalist as "part Cooperstown, a shot of the Rock 'n Roll Hall of Fame with a big
twist of the Smithsonian, to a Beatles soundtrack."

I think that sums up my collection very well. But having
a museum doesn't mean that I've stopped collecting. On
the contrary. I'll be doing this for the rest of my life. Why?
(I think you already know the answer.) Because I... *enjoy
the journey.*

My fondest wish is that you will, too.

Suggested Reading, Viewing, and Other Resources

Websites:

www.collectingwithjeff.com is my website, and it really is worth checking out.

www.nodderexchange.com is John Brey's website about Bobbleheads.

www.worldcollectorsnet.com is an excellent website devoted to collecting.

www.Bonanzle.com is William Harding's excellent website.

www.estatesales.net is Dan McQuade's first rate website about estate sales across the U.S.

www.auctionsniper.com for those last second online bids.

www.lennonhallantiques.com for terrific information on collectibles.

www.npr.org/blogs/politicaljunkie is NPR's Ken Rudin's website. The political junkie has lots about campaign buttons *and* politics in general on his website;

www.apic.org is the website for the American Political Items Collectors.

http://statueoflibertyclub.com is the Statue of Liberty Collector's Club's website.

www.stamps.org/KIDS/kid StampFun.htm is devoted just to stamp collecting children. So is *Junior Philatelists on the Internet* (www.junior-philatelists.com)

www.usmint.gov is the website for the United States Mint.

Books:

Kovels' Antiques and Collectibles Price Guide (for the most recent year available).

Warman's Antiques and Collectibles (for the most recent year available).

Miller's Antiques and Collectibles for the most recent year available).

Price Guide to American Patriotic Memorabilia by Michael Pollok.

Movie Poster Prices by Jon Warren, and *Poster Price Alliance* by John Kisch.

The Card by Michael O'Keefe and Teri Thompson (the Honus Wagner card).

300 Great Baseball Cards of the 20th Century by Mike Piney, and *The Standard Catalog of Baseball Cards* published by Krause Publications.

Secret Identity: The Fetish Art of Superman's Co-creator Joe Shuster.

Petretti's Coca-Cola Collectibles Price Guide.

Dummies series has *Coin Collecting for Dummies* (also *Stamp Collecting for Dummies*).

A Freewheelin' Time: A Memoir of Greenwich Village in the Sixties by Suze Rotolo.

Magazines:

Big Reel (Krause Publications) and/or *Movie Collectors World* (Arena Publication Company) are publications well worth subscribing to.

Beatology Magazine.

Sports Collectors Digest, available as a magazine or –appropriately enough – at sportscollectorsdigest.com.

Video:

Antiques Roadshow, and its PBS companion show *Antiques Roadshow FYI.*

Acknowledgements

One of the distinct pleasures of being a collector is the opportunity to meet and interact with others who also have a passion for collecting. Through the years I have not only shared a great deal with my fellow collectors, but more importantly have made some long term friendships. To these people I wish to expressly give my thanks for helping to inspire me to write this book.

In addition I want to thank Mark Nykanen who helped with the editing and corroboration of this book as well as to Sandra Sauceda and Kathleen Koop who helped with the research and administrative responsibilities.

To the four most important people in my life, my wife Linda, my son Nate, my mother Millie and my late father Harry, thanks for all of your support.

Made in the USA
San Bernardino, CA
19 March 2015